101 MODERN
JAPANESE POEMS

101 MODERN JAPANESE POEMS

Compiled by Makoto Ōoka

Translated by Paul McCarthy

Edited by Janine Beichman

THAMES RIVER PRESS

101 Modern Japanese Poems

THAMES RIVER PRESS
An imprint of Wimbledon Publishing Company Limited (WPC)
Another imprint of WPC is Anthem Press (www.anthempress.com)

First published in the United Kingdom in 2012 by

THAMES RIVER PRESS
75-76 Blackfriars Road
London SE1 8HA

www.thamesriverpress.com

Editorial selection © Makoto Ōoka 2012
English translation © Paul McCarthy 2012
Introduction © Chūei Yagi 2012

This book has been selected by the Japanese Literature Publishing Project (JLPP),
an initiative of the Agency for Cultural Affairs of Japan.

Original title: Gendaishi no kansho 101, compiled by Makoto Ōoka
Copyright © Shinshokan 1998
Originally published in Japan by SHINSHOKAN Co., Ltd., Tokyo

A CIP record for this book is available from the British Library.

ISBN 978-0-85728-558-4

CONTENTS

Preface by Makoto Ōoka   xi

Translator's Note by Paul McCarthy   xiii

Introduction by Chūei Yagi   xv

Hitoshi Oikawa (1913–1996)
    Eyes Straight Ahead. Zigzagging.   1

Yoshirō Ishihara (1915–1977)
    Funeral Train   3
    Ashikaga   4

Saburō Kuroda (1919–1980)
    The Bet   5
    Three O'Clock on an Autumn Afternoon   7
    Birthday   8

Minoru Yoshioka (1919–1990)
    The Past   9
    Monks   10
    Picking Saffron Flowers   14

Sakon Sō (1919–2006)
    Personal History   16

Tsuguo Andō (1919–2002)
    Sleet   19

Masao Nakagiri (1919–1983)
    Personnel Affairs   20

Hitoshi Anzai (1919–1994)
    In the Morning, the Phone Rings   21
    Elevator Mornings   22

Hiroshi Sekine (1920–1994)
    Leaving This Room   23
    A Single Strange Step   24

Rin Ishigaki (1920–2004)
    Shijimi Clams   25
    Name-plates   26
    Land / Houses   27

Nobuo Ayukawa (1920–1986)
    A Morning Song at the Moored Boat Hotel   28
    Heaven   30
    If Now You Suffer   32

Toyoichirō Miyoshi (1920–1992)
    Prisoner   33
    Our Song of a May Night   34

Tarō Naka (1922–)
    Tower   36
    The Sea of Sleep   37

Takayuki Kiyo'oka (1922–2006)
    Alabaster   39
    Through the Ear   40
    An Ecstasy of Sloth   41

Tarō Kitamura (1922–1992)
    Rain   42
    Morning Mirror   43

Ryūichi Tamura (1923–1998)
    Sinking Temple   45
    Etching   46
    The Gods of Poetry   46

Contents

Taka'aki Yoshimoto (1924–)
    Descent to a Singular World   47
    At Tsukuda Ferry   48

Hiroshi Yoshino (1926–)
    I Was Born   50
    Evening Afterglow   51
    Epithalamium   53

Noriko Ibaragi (1926–2006)
    When I Was at My Prettiest   54
    It's Your Own Sensibility   56
    A Tree's Fruit   57

Minoru Nakamura (1927–)
    Night   58
    The Kite   59

Takashi Tsujii (1927–)
    The White Horse   60

Ryūsei Hasegawa (1928–)
    The Laborer's Eyes   62

Eriko Kishida (1929–)
    The Soundless Girl   64
    Why Do Flowers Always   65

Kazue Shinkawa (1929–)
    Don't Bunch Me   66
    Song   67

Hiroshi Kawasaki (1930–2004)
    Swan   68
    Wedding March   69
    Walls of Lead   71

Kōichi Iijima (1930–)
    Understanding   72
    Mother Tongue   73
    The Roads of Miyakojima   74

Chimako Tada (1930–2003)
    First Dream of the New Year   75

Takasuke Shibusawa (1930–1998)
    A Crystal Madness   76
    Ode on Passing through Winter   78

Makoto Ōoka (1931–)
    For Spring   79
    On Place Names   79
    Chōfu V   81

Masami Horikawa (1931–)
    Fresh Pain-filled Days   82

Kazuko Shiraishi (1931–)
    Bird   83
    Penis (for Sumiko's birthday)   85

Toshikazu Yasumizu (1931–)
    The Bird – in four chapters   87

Yasuo Irisawa (1931–)
    Untitled Song   89
    Unidentified Flying Object   90
    Memories of Paradise   91

Shuntarō Tanikawa (1931–)
    Sorrow   92
    An Elaboration of the Way to My House   92
    Mt. Yōkei   94

CONTENTS

Hiroshi Iwata (1932–)
    A Hateful Song   95
    The Ordeal of the Animals   96

Ryōko Shindō (1932–)
    The Plains   98

Sachiko Yoshihara (1932–2002)
    Nonsense   100

Toriko Takarabe (1933–)
    Field Notes at Bakoton, Kitsurin   101

Toshio Nakae (1933–)
    Night and Fish   103
    Vocabulary Collection, Chapter 29   104

Moto'o Andō (1934–)
    A Difficult Walk   106

Taku Miki (1935–)
    A Guest has Come   107

Shirōyasu Suzuki (1935–)
    Confessional-Fiction Virgin Kiki's
        Favorite Form of Play   109
    The Name Sōta   112

Taeko Tomioka (1935–)
    Life Story   113
    Still Life   115

Taijirō Amazawa (1936–)
    Morning River   116
    Counter-Western   116

Mutsuo Takahashi (1937–)
    The Rose Tree   118
    Research on Weeds   119

Tetsuo Shimizu (1938–)
    Charlie Brown   120

Rie Yoshiyuki (1939–2008)
    The Blue Room   121

Yukio Tsuji (1939–2000)
    Kameido   122

Takahiko Okada (1939–1997)
    Borrowing the Name of Love Song   123
    Endure the Splits and Wander On!   124

Hiroshi Osada (1939–)
    How to Eat Radish Wheels   125

Akira Shimizu (1940–)
    Stranded Ship   126

Gōzō Yoshimasu (1939–)
    Burning   128
    First Bath   128

Mikirō Sasaki (1947–)
    Rhododendron Hotel   130

Yōji Arakawa (1949–)
    The Greenery in Mitsuke   132

Hiromi Itō (1955–)
    So as Not to Warp Them   134

List of Sources   137

Index of Poets   142

Index of Titles   143

PREFACE

Makoto Ōoka

This volume introduces 55 leading modern poets of Japan and 101 of their most representative poems. The introduction, specially written by Chūei Yagi, gives an overview of modern Japanese poetry from the immediate postwar period to the present. It provides a superb guide to modern poetry.

The poems included here have been chosen because they reveal the particular qualities of the poets in question. Examples would include the pre-eminent postwar poet Minoru Yoshioka's *Monks*, one of the greatest of modern poetry collections, which begins with the poem "Monks"; "Personnel Affairs" by Masao Nakagiri; "Shijimi Clams" by the thoroughgoing poetic realist Rin Ishigaki; "Don't Bunch Me" by Kazue Shinkawa, who writes of women's sense of being blocked by society; Shuntarō Tanikawa's "Sorrow" (from his collection *Two Billion Light Years of Loneliness*, which was praised as heralding a change in direction in modern poetry); "Untitled Song" by Yasuo Irisawa, who is regarded as the most individual and radically intellectual of modern poets; and "Charlie Brown" by Tetsuo Shimizu, who has published many poems rich in irony and humor. All are first-rate works by their respective creators and all have created a stir in the world of modern poetry.

Most of the poets included here passed through the Pacific War and the postwar period and had various bitter experiences, which formed one of the bases for their works. A representative example would be Nobuo Ayukawa's "A Morning Song at the Moored Boat Hotel," published in 1949, a work written among the postwar ruins, under conditions which could be described only through paradox: "All that is left us is hope."

The poems contained in this volume were written by poets born between 1913 and 1955, the oldest being Hitoshi Oikawa and the youngest Hiromi Itō. Through their works one can sense the movement in poetry that took place from the postwar period to the present.

The first two verses of Hitoshi Oikawa's "Eyes Straight Ahead. Zigzagging.":

> To life with its pointless labours.
> First off, a drink.
>
> Since, when the Uranium Night comes.
> We'll all be very anxious, after all.

And a passage from Hiromi Itō's "So as Not to Warp Them":

> I make them nice and round
> Boil the dumplings, make the syrup, then cool
> Sweet pain
> I fill them with my yearnings
> That thick syrup
> Those smooth white dumplings
> My man gulps them down
> Thick as spittle
> Smooth as buttocks
> How do they taste?

TRANSLATOR'S NOTE

Paul McCarthy

Everyone knows the Italian saying rendered in English as "The translator is a traitor," meaning that he or she must betray either the source language or the target one, or perhaps both, in the course of his/her work. And Robert Frost drily remarked: "Poetry is what gets lost in translation."

So this kind of translation is a challenging task, and one that requires many compromises and adjustments. I hope that I have not proved to be grossly traitorous to either the Japanese or the English, and that something of the poetry of the original survives; but that is for each reader to decide. For those who can read Japanese, the information about the original titles of the poems and the volumes in which they appeared and, wherever possible, about places and dates of publication should prove helpful.

Japanese poetry has no tradition of rhyming. Given the phonetics of the language, rhyming would be too simple a technique to be interesting. Traditional Japanese poetry relies on syllable count for its metrics, but this system has been almost entirely abandoned in the writing of modern-style poetry, although it is maintained in the writing of traditional tanka, haiku and the like. The postwar poets represented in this collection almost never rely on syllable count.

Several elements remain, and are of signal importance, however. First, there is the sheer sound and feel of the poetry. Since the sound systems of English and Japanese are so different, no exact equivalence can be attempted. But if the language is everyday and straightforward in Japanese, one can try to find a comparable style in English. An example would be Rin Ishigaki's "Name-plates." Yet if the Japanese original is "rich and strange," one must try to do something similar in the target language. An example would be Takasuke Shibusawa's "Ode on Passing through Winter." In a very few cases, the whole point of a poem has been sound values: strings of words that are similar in sound in the original, "poem as extended pun" and the like. If it was judged that the point of a poem would be not merely blunted, but lost in translation, substitutions were, regretfully, made, as the reader who compares the English version of the text with the Japanese original poem by poem will discover.

Imagery is of prime importance, and I have tried to reproduce the original images used, staying close to the order in which they are presented whenever English syntax permits. Minoru Yoshioka's famous and controversial poem "Monks" progresses through a series of stark, shocking images, as does his "Picking Saffron Flowers," though to very different effect.

One feature of some of the poems in this anthology that may puzzle the English reader is the use of spacing within the lines of a poem. These *ma*, to use a common Japanese term, do not have a grammatical or syntactical function, but may indicate where the poet wants the reader to pause, at least mentally, as he reads. They may represent the "breath" of the poem. Or they may visually break up the line in a way that the poet finds pleasing. One thinks of the creative use of empty space in classical Japanese painting and calligraphy. An attempt has been made to reproduce most of these *ma* in roughly the same places in the line where they occur, though the constraints of the English poetic line have sometimes made exact equivalence impossible. I would like to express my thanks to the meticulous editors at Thames River Press, who have made every effort to accommodate this unfamiliar patterning of lines in the present volume.

The reader of this anthology will, I am sure, be struck by the extraordinary diversity of themes, styles, stances and diction. Men and women poets, those who show greater affinities with the earlier Japanese poetic tradition and those who are consciously responding to contemporary movements in European and American poetry, socially engaged poets and those who seem immersed in private systems of thought or fantasy, bleakly tragic poets and insouciantly comic ones – all are represented.

Many people have helped me with this translation, though the final responsibility is mine. I would like to mention in particular Mr. Fuminori Abe of Fukuoka Prefecture and Professor Janine Beichman of Tokyo, who carefully read both the originals and my translations. Their help has been invaluable.

Spring 2012
Tokyo

INTRODUCTION: THE WINDING ROAD
OF MODERN JAPANESE POETRY

Chūei Yagi

The beginnings of modern Japanese poetry can be traced to *New Style Poems* (1882) by Shōichi Toyama, Ryōkichi Yatabe, et al. This collection mostly contained translations of European poetry, with only five original poems by Toyama and his colleagues. The style of these original poems was very different from what we have nowadays come to think of as modern poetry.

Twenty-two years later, Tōson Shimazaki announced the arrival of a new age in poetry with the famous words: "At last the time for a new poetry has come, like a beautiful dawn..." (Preface to *The Poetry of Tōson Shimazaki*). And indeed one can sense elements of "a beautiful dawn" in his poetic sensibility, with its new lyricism and feel for language.

I have no space to discuss in detail the poetry of the period from 1882 to 1945, generally known in Japan as "early modern poetry." Many early modern poets, including such representative figures as Sakutarō Hagiwara, Kenji Miyazawa, Hakushū Kitahara, Kōtarō Takamura, and Chūya Nakahara, are still devotedly read, discussed, and studied by large numbers of people today. Some of the older poets included in this volume began reading these earlier poets in their youth, during the decade of the mid-1930s to the mid-1940s, and began writing their own poetry at around the same time. (The poets included in this volume were all born between 1913 and 1955, it should be pointed out.)

The terms "early modern" and "modern" as they relate to Japanese poetry are, as is so often the case with historical labels, ambiguous. The period after Japan's defeat in World War II in 1945 is usually called "postwar," and the poetry written then is called "postwar poetry" or "modern poetry." Poetry written prior to the defeat is termed "early modern;" however, the poetry of the Meiji and Taishō periods (1868–1925) is also sometimes called "early modern."

The Fifteen-Year War extending from 1931 to 1945 – beginning with the Manchurian Incident, continuing with the Second

Sino-Japanese War, and culminating in World War II – was for the Japanese an unprecedented experience of war and defeat. With the unconditional surrender that ended the war in 1945, the Japanese were utterly devastated, physically and spiritually.

During that long war, writers and poets were mobilized along with the rest of the nation, and forced to cooperate in the war effort in various ways. And this was not only in direct, physical ways: many leading poets were made to write poems glorifying the war and the nation's will to fight – in short, "war-support poems." After the war there was heated debate about these war poems. Literary men, like sports professionals, were sent off to the battlefield to die in combat, or died of illness in the field, or had to flee after defeat, or were taken prisoner – many shared this kind of bitter fate. Yet it is true that such experiences helped produce literary works of very high quality, including numerous poems. Japan's unconditional surrender also marked the beginning of Japan's postwar literature and poetry.

"Modern poetry," in contradistinction to "early modern poetry," was often called "postwar poetry" as well. Recently, however, some sixty years after the end of the war, we rarely hear the term "postwar poetry," as is only natural. Various ideas that cannot be bundled together with terms like "war," "defeat," or "postwar" are now in general circulation, and not only among young poets. In the early 1960s one often heard people say, "We're not living in the postwar period anymore." But even that very sentiment now seems behind the times. Indeed, there are voices warning that we are now in a new "prewar" period.

Taka'aki Yoshimoto, one of the most logically analytical of modern poetry critics and himself an excellent poet, has written: "Japan's modern poetry clearly showed, as it emerged from the Second World War, that the realm of the poetic imagination had no poetry strong enough to exist in isolation from its social milieu… The emergence of the postwar poets was a new indicator of what the experience of war had added to the personal imaginative power of Japan's modern poetry" ("On the History of Postwar Poetry").

The first of these observations expresses disappointment with the poetry prior to the Second World War (early modern poetry), while the second expresses appreciation of the postwar poets. Yoshimoto goes on to ask if there were any postwar poets who saw Japan's defeat as a kind of liberation, and concludes that likely none did. In the "disappointment," then, lay the fateful point of departure for the postwar poets.

Among the poems contained in this anthology, the first to be written in the postwar period was Nobuo Ayukawa's "A Morning Song at the Moored Boat Hotel," published in a magazine in January 1949. It is one of the most representative of the numerous postwar poems, and it bitterly rejects the modernism that can be sensed in prewar poetry.

In his postwar essay "The Spirit of a Man Without a Country," Ayukawa wrote:

"There's nothing in Japan now that may be undertaken in a half-hearted, mediocre way. We must build up everything thoroughly, from the very beginning. We should burn down the little that has remained from the conflagration. We should start everything again from the ashes. At least this is the case for us as we begin to write our poetry."

And Ryūichi Tamura, who belonged to the same Wasteland Group of poets as Nobuo Ayukawa, wrote as follows in his well-known poem "Upright in the Coffin":

> We have no country on this earth
> No country on this earth that is worth our lives.

Tarō Kitamura, also of the Wasteland Group, wrote: "Our pockets are empty." All of them were young people (with at least one woman) in their early twenties, and all experienced a deep sense of loss and were forced to start again in the emptiness of the postwar period.

As I quote these lines from their poems and consider the kinds of poetry and other discourses being produced in Japan nowadays, I am tempted to say: "My, but we've come an awfully long way!" That's how big a gap has emerged (naturally enough) between the early "postwar poetry" and contemporary works. And yet, on the contrary, I cannot repress the feeling that we have, in reality, taken only a very few steps forward.

Apart from the poets mentioned above, the Wasteland Group had as its principal members Saburō Kuroda, Masao Nakagiri, and Toyoichirō Miyoshi. The Archipelago Group took a different stance, with clear societal concerns. Its core members were Hiroshi Sekine, Gan Tanikawa, Yoshio Kuroda, and Ryūsei Hasegawa. It is possible to distinguish the two groups in a schematized way, going back to the pre-war division between the Modernists and the Proletarian Poets; but in fact, with the passage of time, the differences between the two postwar groups have grown less and less meaningful.

The word "wasteland" in that group's name goes back to T. S. Eliot's great poem, and both the Modernists and the Proletarian Poets of the prewar period were inevitably subject to European influences in one way or another, as they followed their various winding paths. Yet in general these European influences did not put down deep roots in Japan. A Modernist like Junzaburō Nishiwaki – who studied in England and had an extraordinary cultural background – or a Surrealist like Shūzō Takiguchi were exceptional cases, each of them leaving behind a superior body of work. However, neither the Archipelago Group nor the Four Seasons Group, which emphasized lyricism, bore much fruit as major movements, though there were exceptional individual poets in each group.

Lyricism was at the very root of Japan's poetry, the history of which is pervaded by a traditional poetic spirit that celebrates the beauties of nature – and this is especially true of the medieval waka form. It is hard to discuss the Japanese poetic tradition without reference to its attitude toward nature, its dialogue with nature. Moreover, the emphasis on the beauties of nature was not just confined to the realm of poetry (especially waka and haiku); it lived on as a powerful and wide-ranging spirit through the long history of Japanese arts like the tea ceremony and flower arrangement, and it continues to do so today. It was deeply and inseparably related to the Japanese way of life and aesthetic sense, passing beyond the bounds of poetry and other formal arts.

The history of early modern poetry centers on the attempt to celebrate "a time of new poetry" like that which Tōson Shimazaki described as "a beautiful dawn." It was truly "an age of song." In contrast, it is often said that postwar poetry was not engaged in mere "singing" and its accompanying pleasurable feelings, but was rather the product of "an age of thought." And this is true, if we wish make a simple contrast between the two periods.

> The country is ruined, the mountains and rivers remain.
> Spring has come to the capital, the grasses and trees are deep.
> (Du Fu, "A Spring View")

These "mountains and rivers," however, are already wasteland, and only the grasses and trees are trying vainly to announce the coming of spring. This eighth-century poem by Du Fu, describing the devastation of the Tang capital of Chang'an after a war, transcends the divide of nations and periods and serves to describe Japan in defeat after World War II.

In an earlier introduction to the Japanese edition of the present anthology, Makoto Ōoka comments on Nobuo Ayukawa's "A Morning Song at the Moored Boat Hotel": "This poem has as its immediate background such things as…the impoverished scene of postwar Japan, the defeated nation's very innards spilled out for all to see, and the kind of life that had to be led under such conditions – a feeling of vast spatial and temporal emptiness that could only be expressed paradoxically in the statement 'All that is left to us is hope.'"

Ayukawa, whose poem occasioned these observations, himself clearly states regarding the writing of poetry: "Individuality doesn't accomplish much. Neither gradual advances nor dramatic leaps can be expected from poets who rely on the lyrical quality of language and use words as tools to express the atmosphere of nature and the emotions aroused by it."

"A Morning Song at the Moored Boat Hotel" contains the lines

> The view from the window
> Is set within a frame
> Ah, I long for rain and city-streets and night

Ayukawa wants the view from the window to be of "rain," "city-streets," and "night," all of which should have a latent atmosphere of lyricism; but these are lacking, and the poet's desire remains unfulfilled. This represented a kind of irony, and it was not so much "the view from the window" of Nobuo Ayukawa as it was "the view from the window" of the Japanese who had emerged from the prewar and wartime periods into the postwar one.

From the day of the defeat, the Japanese were suddenly forced to reverse all the value judgments informing their lives. The emperor, whom the common people had been taught to believe in and worship as "a deity in human form," turned overnight into "an ordinary human being." "Wartime poetry," which had seemed so strong and bold, was immediately dragged down among the ashes of defeat. We have already quoted Taka'aki Yoshimoto to the effect that the realm of poetic imagination within modern Japanese poetry proved not to have created poems strong enough to exist apart from their "social milieu." Both poems and poets were swayed by the "social milieu" in which they stood as they lived through the wartime era. The defeat in World War II was a decisive collapse, the first of its kind in Japanese history; at the same time it marked the beginning of a period filled with feelings of liberation, together with unparalleled cultural and social confusion.

I may have seemed to pay too much attention to the period around the war's end, but I have my reasons for doing so. When we discuss modern Japanese poetry (postwar poetry), the poets' experiences of war and defeat inevitably become a major factor. And this is true, of course, not only for modern poetry but for all sorts of areas, from postwar politics, economics, culture, and education all the way to sports.

In February 1946, six months after the war's end, Makoto Ōoka, then a fifteen-year-old junior in middle school, together with several of his classmates put out the initial issue of a magazine called *Demon's Words*. It signified the appearance of poets "without the wounds of war," those who had been too young to be sent to the battlefield. Among several early poems written by Ōoka in that year was one entitled "To a Persimmon Tree," which includes the following lines:

> In the fall of last year
> No fruit ripened
> Had you despaired
> At the sorrows of war?
> The three or four small fruits that appeared
> Fell without ripening red
> But this year
> Your breath of new life
> Floods the flowers in bloom

This is written in traditional literary language and takes the form of a lament, but what is notable is that it leaves behind "the sorrows of war" and presents the "breath of new life" and "flowers in bloom" before our eyes. It should be clear to the reader what the persimmon tree that is trying to bear fruit this year symbolizes.

In Ōoka's early poems from the same period we find lively, highly positive expressions like "What a pleasant time that was!" ("Summer Arrives"), "Oh words loudly chanted!" ("Illusion"), "The earth, overflowing with the joy of morning" ("Morning Ode"), and

"A joyous band of girls" ("Forest"). This is not mere frivolity or easy optimism. The joy of being released at last from a dark, depressing era had begun to fill the hearts and bodies of the young, and with it, hope. Naturally enough, a very different consciousness and sensibility from that of Nobuo Ayukawa, Ryūichi Tamura and other poets of the previous generation were starting to emerge. Then Shuntarō Tanikawa burst forth onto the literary stage with the shocking collection *Two Billion Light Years of Loneliness*, giving Japan a dazzling poetic voice of a sort it had not had until then. Other young poets of Makoto Ōoka's generation, including Hiroshi Kawasaki, Kazuko Shiraishi, Yasuo Irisawa, Kōichi Iijima, and Hiroshi Iwata, appeared, expressing contemporary realities in their various styles. All of them vividly reflected the new age that bore no scars from the war, and they began to create a new ground swell in modern Japanese poetry.

Shuntarō Tanikawa published *Two Billion Light Years of Loneliness* in 1952, when he was twenty-one. The critic Kiwao Nomura's observation that "this was an event which announced the first real change in direction for modern poetry in Japan" is by no means an overstatement: it truly was "an event." It represented a new departure in modern poetry, a direction that had not existed in the poetic genetic code up to then. Tanikawa's volume was greeted with a great sense of shock not only in the poetic world but in the postwar literary world in general. Tanikawa went on to transcend the genre of modern poetry and became active over a broad spectrum, creating children's songs and stories, works based on word-play, illustrated books, films, and dramas – activities that he continues to this day. At the root of all of these activities is the consciousness and receptivity of a true genius – a poetic mind whose waves beat constantly but variously. As modern poetry's foremost leader, Tanikawa continues his energetic activities, always inspired by fresh ideas. It is no exaggeration to say that he is a "super-poet" who surpasses even that early-modern poet known to all Japanese, Hakushū Kitahara.

Nor can we forget another poet, Yasuo Irisawa, one of the most outstanding of our artists, who has continued to broaden with great boldness the possibilities of the field of modern poetry. Using his keen intellect and free-ranging thought, he has continued interrogating the possibilities of poetry, even beyond its normal bounds. He is at present the most radically intellectual of our poets. The opening poem in his first collection *Happy or Unhappy* (1955) is entitled

"Untitled Song," well expressing his defiance of convention. And the poem itself is structured in such a way that the ambiguous, somehow indecent-sounding refrain "jajanka waiwai" echoes throughout the whole piece.

Irisawa also wrote the well-known long poem titled "My Izumo, My Requiem" (1968), which has a notably complex and contrived structure. The poem was published with a massive collection of Irisawa's notes appended to it, which was roughly equal in volume to the poem itself; this appendix set itself over and against the poem in a way that defied common sense. Thus "My Izumo, My Requiem" became both by reputation and in reality a work on an extraordinary, hitherto unknown scale.

And once, for a particular anthology, the poets included were asked to comment on their own works. Yasuo Irisawa's sole comment was "Poetry is anger." I cannot have been the only reader who gasped when reading this. But after a moment's reflection, I came to the conclusion, "How very like Yasuo Irisawa!"

One more anecdote: there was a weekly magazine called *Asahi Journal* that was widely read by intellectuals and students, and it decided to feature modern poetry in each issue for a period of one year, beginning 1 January 1971. In the 1 January issue, Yasuo Irisawa contributed a poem entitled "A Plaintive Prologue." He used a different ideogram to write the last part of his personal name, but everyone knew of course that it was he. The text of the poem consisted of 20 repetitions of the single line: "In today's Japan, poetry has been totally humiliated." Even now I cannot forget the great shock I received at the repetition of this one line. Was it in fact a poem? The literal meaning of the line was something that any sensitive Japanese poet of the time could totally agree with. "Humiliated" here had a profound, and by no means simple, meaning. In this one line, with cynical directness, Irisawa touched the very core of modern Japanese poetry's contemporary state. He was asking us, his readers, "Well then, what do *you* think of this country and its poetry?"

I have no space here to examine in detail the profundity or the manifold aspects of this poem's meaning. Undoubtedly Irisawa was engaging in conscious mischief-making here, but that was by no means the whole of it. He was not merely stressing his own conceptual or structural eccentricity. He is an extremely intelligent poet, rare in his analytic tendency; if modern poetry is in general difficult to understand, he must be placed at the ultima Thule of difficulty. The field of modern poetry has been enlarged and deepened by Yasuo Irisawa.

Moving from "early modern" to "modern poetry," Japanese poetry emerged from the sad and bitter experience of the war and immediate postwar period and – with the appearance of numerous younger postwar poets – has gradually come to take as its main theme the peaceful everyday life of ordinary people. In a sense, the experience of the war and the bitterness of defeat have undeniably weathered with the passage of time. People's ways of living and thinking and the structure of society and the economy have become more heterogeneous in complex ways, as is only natural.

The problem for poetry is how to interact with the present heterogeneous age – how to be receptive to its various elements, digest them as a "language universe," and then express them adequately. This is not a task to be easily accomplished by just anyone. I wrote above of "the peaceful everyday life of ordinary people"; but a simplistic phrase like "peaceful everyday life" does not really hold true in the realm of poetry. Modern poetry is ceaselessly changing along with the currents of the age, and it does so with a tremendous, almost dizzying energy that will no doubt lead to great transformations. Putting the matter simply, we can say that postwar poetry has been a history of Japan's transformation in the direction of heterogeneity.

The 55 poets included in this collection are all certainly representative of modern poetry in Japan – this seems objectively true. Their 101 poems must of course await the judgment of the reader, but I can say that great efforts have been made to select works that well express each poet's special character. Thus, for example, Minoru Yoshioka's "Monks," Masao Nakagiri's "Personnel Affairs," Rin Ishigaki's "Shijimi Clams," Hiroshi Yoshino's "I Was Born," Kazuko Shiraishi's "Penis," Hiroshi Iwata's "A Hateful Song," Shirōyasu Suzuki's "Confessional-Fiction Virgin Kiki's Favorite Form of Play," Tetsuo Shimizu's "Charlie Brown," and Yōji Arakawa's "The Greenery in Mitsuke" all met with strong reactions when they were first published, roused debate, and became landmarks in modern poetry. And I can assure the reader that the works of the other poets also represent their respective poetic oeuvres. They have built up the geological strata of modern Japanese poetry; they are part of the motive energy that formed its groundswells.

Modern poetry has transformed itself in accordance with the changes in the age, yet poets have had to keep resisting the pressure to pander to mere popular taste and yield to convention. This natural resistance has led to a history of poetic struggle that has lasted for over sixty years since the war's end, and its fruits can be seen in the present anthology. And of course the struggle of modern poetry continues even now. In the history of that struggle, there have been many unfortunate complications and dangerous pitfalls. Not a few poets have wandered into blind alleys that were hard to exit.

Recently a new trend toward rhetorical ambiguity has appeared among the younger generation of poets in particular. Even if one wished to sing of the beauties of nature nowadays, the traditional beauties have vanished from our everyday lives. In order to sing in this way, the poet must seek out uniquely contemporary forms of natural beauty, and exercise his or her creativity through them. The general public complains, as before, of modern poetry's "isolation from society" and "difficulty." How poets are to understand their present situation and respond to it presents a grave problem.

Taka'aki Yoshimoto, who understands the poetic present as "a rhetorical present," writes: "It is meaningless to make distinctions between poets in terms of the ground of their sensibility or the characteristic quality of their thought. What distinguishes one poet from another is language, rhetorical concerns." Yoshimoto goes on to say that this rhetoric of which he speaks is not so much a matter of "schools" or "groups" of poets as it is a generational trend.

These observations of Yoshimoto's were made some thirty years ago, and they evoked much sympathy and became a major topic in poetic circles. He was talking mainly about the works of poets who began being active from the 1960s onwards (i.e., the last 10 to 15 poets in the present anthology). The trend toward "rhetorical concerns" to which he refers has in fact gained strength in the works of Hiromi Itō (the last poet included here) and her younger fellow poets. Will this trend make the field of modern Japanese literature a still more fertile and productive place, or will it invite new crises? For the answer to these questions, we will have to wait and see.

Eyes Straight Ahead. Zigzagging.

To life with its pointless labors.
First off, a drink.

Since, when the Uranium Night comes.
We'll all be very anxious, after all.

Yakitori, stewed giblets, chilled tofu.
I wish it was roast lamb from the Chengyang Restaurant in
    Chengyangmen-wai.

Lately, times are tough.
As you well know, we're not on easy street.

To celebrate our high spirits for the nonce.
Surely this is the only way.

After one drink, one more.
And after that, another.

Till our stomachs can't take it anymore.
There's nothing for it but to drink.

Brothers. Drink up.
There's nothing like "nothing like drinking."

The times are truly ominous.
The flags of both sides flap-flap, flap-flap.

But what a bore for all of us.
We'll never be flag-bearers.

All the more, then. Still more. Indeed.
We like things hot and bitter.

Beyond being beyond being beyond being dead drunk.
We're on our way to a spot that's soft and warm.

To Vagina   Uterus   our Cradle-tomb.
We. Eyes straight ahead. Zigzagging.

(*The Rotgut Anthology*, 1955)

YOSHIRŌ ISHIHARA (1915–1977)

Funeral Train

From what station have we come?
No one remembers anymore
Only   to the right it's always broad daylight
To the left midnight
Through this strange land
The train keeps running
When we arrive at some station   always
A red lamp peers through the window
Along with dirty wooden legs and battered shoes
Pitch-black lumps of something are thrown in
They're all alive
Even as the train chugs onward
They go on living but
Still inside the cars
The stench of death is everywhere
I am there too
All are half-ghosts by now
They lean against each other and
As their bodies rub against the others
They eat and drink
A little still but
There are some whose buttocks have become transparent
About to disappear
O I am there too
Leaning bitterly against the window
One of us bites now and then
Into a rotten apple
Me?   Or my ghost?
And so we often
Lie upon our ghosts
Or move away from them
Meanwhile we wait for the train to arrive
At an unbearable distant future
Who is in the engine-room?

Each time we cross a giant black steel bridge
The bridge-piers rumble
Many ghosts rest their hands
From eating
Trying to remember
From what station have we come?

(Sancho Panza's Return, 1963)

Ashikaga

Over the town of Ashikaga
An umbrella crossed the sky
Crossed, impossibly, the azure sky
And dropped upon the ground
A round shadow like a greeting
People stopped one after the other
Gazing silently at
The surface of the street that
On that one spot alone
Grew round and wet

(Ashikaga, 1977)

The Bet

Say I got a wife with a five million yen dowry
What would a pauper like me do?
Buy a piano, drink some booze
Kiss behind the curtains
What else?
Say I got a wife, beautiful, wise, and chaste
What would a boozer like me do?
Hold her like a new silk hat in these hands
And not know what to do
What else?

O
Then
The world went silent
On this white building's second floor
I saw
Foolish
Just like me
Poor, moody
Stubborn
A Jacobsen rose at her breast
Both eyes full of the sadness of unbelief
Spitting out sharp words
Like grape seeds
Two deep dimples next to her lips
I saw
A girl

The biggest gamble of my life
And what should I have bet?
Turning out my pockets
Plucking out
The chance of a five million yen dowry

A poet's laurels, unpaid bills
A torn-off button
Everything
So
Though I turn my coin-purse upside down and shake it hard
I've nothing to bet
I
Bet my ruin
My ruin
As the world went silent
Like a first-time gambler
I opened my closed eyes

(*To a Woman*, 1954)

Three O'Clock on an Autumn Afternoon

Sitting on a bench by Shinobazu Pond
Stealthily I open a pint of whiskey
Little Yuri dressed in her best
Runs straight across the white sand
Then circles back

In the distance sea lions bark wildly
"Kwa-Kwa-Kwa"
Little Yuri imitating the sound as she returns
Three o'clock on an autumn afternoon
On the other bank where ducks are gathered
A few people

Far off, faint sounds of autos' horns
Everything far off
Like a far-off, distant world
I look at two shadows lined up on the white sand
Shadows of a father shirking his day's work
And of his little daughter

(*With Little Yuri*, 1960)

Birthday

My fiftieth birthday
Spent flat on my back with a slipped disk
Outside, the sound of a bull-dozer
From far away, children's voices
Sometimes a dog barks
A distant world

By my pillow
A new volume of my poems
Enfolded in kind words
From acquaintances and friends
Lightly there
My life

No matter how wretched
No matter how petty
It is my life
I have no other
But now
With just that there before me
My heart is heavy

If my mind
Were scattered in disorder
If I could lose myself in the noises of the world
If that were so
How refreshed I would feel

Walking the Musashino woods till tired
With a flask of sake and a bowl of soba
Forgetting myself
If it were so
How happy I would be
Flat on my back with a slipped disk
On my birthday

(From "The Footsteps of a Sheep,"
Saburō Kuroda Poetry Anthology, 1970)

MINORU YOSHIOKA (1919–1990)

The Past

He first hangs his cook's garb from his scrawny neck
He has no past, as he has no will
He starts to walk with a sharp blade in one hand
A file of ants races by, reflected in the corner of his open eye
Lit by the double-bladed knife, the dust upon the floor begins to
    rustle
The item to be cooked
Were it even a toilet bowl
Would let out a scream, no doubt
Would shed its blood at once from the window out toward the sun
Something quietly awaits him now
Something that will grant him
The past that he has lacked
On the block a stingray lies, unmoving
Its great wet speckled back
Its tail hanging down, it seems, as far as the cellar
Beyond, only roofs under winter rain
Swiftly he rolls up his sleeves
And sticks the blade into the flesh of the stingray's gut
No resistance
In slaughter
No reaction
No dirtying of hands is a fearful thing
But he pushes harder bit by bit, slitting open the membranous space
Dark depths from which nothing comes forth
Stars that now appear, now fade away
Work done, he takes his hat from off the wall
Goes out the door
A portion that his hat had hid till now

The nail mark guarded from great fear
From it blood, replete with the heaviness and roundness of
    sufficient time,
Flows slowly down

(*Still-life*, 1955)

Monks

1.

Four monks
Strolling in the garden
Occasionally rolling up their black cloths
Shapes of rods
Hitting at a young woman
Without any malice
Until bats screech
One makes dinner
One searches for a sinner
One masturbates
One is killed by the woman

2.

Four monks
Hard at work on their tasks
Taking down the sacred dolls
Hoisting a cow upon a cross
One shaves another's head
The dead one says a prayer
When another makes a coffin
A flood of child-births sweeps in from the village at dead of
    night
The four all rise together
Four crippled umbrellas
Beautiful walls and ceiling
A hole appears there
Rain begins to fall

3.

Four monks
Sit down at the dinner table
The one with long arms passes out the forks
Another's warted hand pours out the wine
The other two do not show their hands
Touching a cat of today and
A woman of the future
Their hands build up a hairy figure
With the bodies of both
Flesh is what binds the bones together
Flesh is what is exposed in blood
Two are fat from gluttony
Two are scrawny from creating

4.

Four monks
Go out for their morning ascesis
One goes as a bird to the forest to welcome a hunter
One goes as a fish to the river to peek at a serving-maid's thighs
One bears as a horse from the town the tools of slaughter
One is dead so he rings the bell
The four have never loudly laughed

5.

Four monks
Sowing seeds in a field
One by mistake
Offers a turnip to the buttocks of a child
The mouth of the porcelain-faced mother, all amazed
A sunken reddish muddy sun
Riding on a swing that goes so high
The three monks sing in chorus
The one that's dead
Gives voice inside the deep throat of a nesting crow

6.

Four monks
Squat around a well
The laundry includes the scrotum of a goat
Sanitary cloths too numerous to wash
All three together wring out
A sheet as large as a blimp
The dead one lugs it out to dry
On top of the steeple in the rain

7.

Four monks
One writes the history of the abbey and the private stories of
    the four
One writes about the lives of flowery queens throughout the
    world
One writes the history of monkeys, axes, tanks
One is dead so
Hiding from the other three
He burns their records one by one

8.

Four monks
One fathered a thousand bastards in a land of withered trees
One killed a thousand bastards in a saltless moonless sea
One, on a scale where snakes and grapes are intertwined
Was surprised to see the feet of a thousand dead and the eyes
    of a thousand living weighed the same
One was dead but still unwell
Coughing there beyond the wall of stone

9.

Four monks
Leave the fortress of their hard breastplates
The harvest of their lives is nothing so
In a place one stage higher than the world
They hang themselves, laughing together
That's why
The bones of the four, thick as winter trees
Hang dead there until an age when the rope will snap

(*Monks*, 1958)

Picking Saffron Flowers

On the wall of a royal palace in Crete
There is, they say, a gorgeous fresco called
"Picking Saffron Flowers"
There   a boy down on all fours
Is picking saffron flowers
Days when between the rocks
        blue waves repeat their swirling patterns
But, though we only see him from the rear,
If on the boy's brow   the sun should fall
Grains of salt, star-shaped, appear
When on the promontory at dusk
The boy's cleft buttocks
Are thrust out
We   recognize the dripping of the fragrant sap
        from a saffron flower's stalk
Waves come   Whitecaps
Next decapitated
A beautiful monkey's head will be displayed
Upon the quartz-like face
Of the boy, eyes shut, plunged deep in darkness
Like the portrait of Arcimboldo
Made from spring fruits and fish
All decomposes
From the surface down
Night when the virgin's skin is irresistible
The monkey's torso tawed
By faith and curses beneath the Aegean Sea
Dead blue fur trembling
Do the boy's damp shoulders hold aloft
The thighs of his wet nurse?
Or the monkey's hidden penis?
It is reflected in a great mirror
Like an ideograph
The twilight starts to dye the distant pillars
The disappearing waves
Go round and round inside brown-colored spiral shells
"Song" is born

Faint purple of the saffron flower
If there is one who summons
The boy will run down the rocky ledges,
Borrowing from among so many apparent deaths
    the shape of death by drowning
For now   we will say nothing
Must say nothing
Of the legend of the swimming monkey
Until the canopy of heaven
Is covered by the waves

(Picking Saffron Flowers, 1976)

SAKON SŌ (1919–2006)

Personal History

Volcanic ash spumes forth from great Mt. Aso
Burying deep the history of warriors' plunder/ murder from
    Nara, Heian, Genkō, Kemmu
In sleeping Waifu Town, Kikuchi County, Kumamoto
Wood shacks, drenched with spray fresh from Kikuchi River,
    like urine spurted out toward the sun
By colts that free in pastures run
Begin to rot and lean and sink away
In a corner of the dark silkworm room in a dirt-poor
    peasant's house
In 1887 when the brown memories of the Seinan War had
    dimmed
In dirty winter when the fallen autumn leaves were mired in muck
A baby, somehow spared infanticide, survived
An infant with one older brother, two older sisters, a younger
    sister and a brother each
A girl who must be nurse to the younger and servant to the
    older ones
Not even one day of school allowed
Only counting pebbles by the shore, sobbing, crying, playing
When the sun goes down she works the loom and sometimes
    falls asleep upon it
From twelve until nineteen, the valleys of the Chinese and
    Russian wars,
Selling flowers near the Nagasaki Mitsubishi shipyard
1911, and a son is born, a love-child
Acknowledged by Uemura X, the priest of Temple Y, in Z Town,
    Nagasaki, but
Come 1912, a new age dawns, the start of Taisho's reign – he cuts
    her off
1916, she takes her son and goes to wed
One Koga Ushinosuke, a ruined wandering gambler twenty years
    her senior
1919, the First of May, a son is newly born

Mother
This is all I know
Of your life till I was born
How you spent your girlhood
Why you separated from that first man
What kind of loves and dreams you had, and lost
First you and then your brothers and your sisters
Saying nothing, turned your backs and passed to the other shore
My older brother still remains but
I cannot bring myself to question him and
He himself seems not to want to talk
Most likely he and I, so long as we both live
Would no more touch upon your life
Than intrude upon your tomb
Mother
Just because I was so weak
A sudden mutation among our relatives, from an endless line
    of poor peasants
Who drank bitter mud like pond snails, silent as the dead,
Just because I could not act as sitter, servant or rice-
    field hand
I'm wandering here in distant Paris, farther even than your
    Nagasaki
Mother
I wouldn't want to be the Dean of Notre Dame Cathedral
I'd like to be a scrap-metal dealer who
Smashes Notre Dame to bits and sells it off
Mother
Do you know what I'd want to leave unsmashed until the end?
The gargoyle rain-spouts on the eaves
Those ghosts
That spit out that which they themselves have never drunk
Those ghosts
Them
I'd like slowly to strike until they break
The sedimented mud that's not their own
That's seeped into their very bodies
I'd like slowly to dissect
Mother

Your life
Your life which no one tells me of
Created just to pass along and flow away
This ghost that is myself
I'd like to slowly strike until it breaks

(*My Mother, Burning*, 1967)

TSUGUO ANDŌ (1919–2002)

Sleet

Before reaching the ground
A premonitory
Turning point
From there
Putrefied dead times
Begin
When the wind stretches the membranes
The sun warms this imitation egg
The water that escapes into the sky and
The fish that fall from out of that water
Are my neuralgia
The fish that broke through the interfering weir
Have become ungatherable white bones
And are scattered through the world
At that time people
Recall so many words that look like "tears" –
    as, "teas," "ears", "stare", "rates" –
But never are quite "tears"

(February)

(*CALENDRIER*, 1960)

MASAO NAKAGIRI (1919–1983)

Personnel Affairs

"Our branch's next sub-head—it's you, for sure!"
Watching the reaction, he flatters away.
The other beams with joy:
"Oh, have another drink!" and offers a small cup.

"Our section-chief has no idea how to handle people!"
"They say he'll never make department-head."
All Japan's a company, and
Personnel affairs are all you hear over evening drinks.

At last they say goodnight, they're on their own
The night-time breeze of early spring caresses every cheek
They sober up and feel alone
They kick at empty packs of cigarettes, and stones.

Yet they had dreams when they were young
And certain small ideals, until they joined the company.

(*Personnel Affairs*, 1979)

HITOSHI ANZAI (1919–1994)

In the Morning, the Phone Rings

The phone rings as I start the washing-machine
It's him – only his upper half has left the night behind
With a buzz as from some distant sawmill
He rubs the shaver over his face and says the same old things:
"Had a good night's sleep all on my own here in the apartment;
Sure like to have some of your ham and eggs"
Oh? and who is that, then?
Her back to you, facing the wall
Just now slipping on her bra…
If you didn't call, you wouldn't be found out
But on mornings when there is no call I'm a broken washing-
    machine
I'm proud of me
I work so hard
Briskly making new each yesterday
I love to spread fine weather in the garden
The children are long gone to school, blown and scattered by the
    wind
My husband's already on the bus, frowning face above stiff collar
He takes me out to some dull place once in ten days or so
Then sticks his finger in my ear, my mouth, just anywhere
And turns me inside out.

(*A Handsome Man*, 1958)

Elevator Mornings

When I want to meet her, off I go
Pushing an arm through one sleeve in the elevator
As I descend the building's spine
I need you here! the phone says, choking off the rest
Twisting myself round in the swivel chair I stand
And rush off looking fresh
As if I've just emerged from some green thicket
Straight on I go, car spattering through rain and mud
She waits, pretending to be napping
Beside the garden's pepper tree
Always hung with melancholy bells
She wants to be surprised on opening her eyes
When with the woman that I love, I'm talkative
But in her presence I never speak badly of my friends
If she sends word she's returning from a trip
I'll not wait lazily on the terminus platform
But go instead to the rural station one before
Tap her shoulder there on the "racing morning train"
Her suitcase on the rack above
Is oh-so heavy
And I have to lend a hand
I'm close-mouthed, though, about my love-affairs
I'm good at keeping small promises like that
"Never put off 'til tomorrow what you can do today" – my creed
And yet, with only that to boast about
They'll never let me join the Party, like my friend
I'll never get to be a "secret Party member" anywhere
My one affair is with a favorite woman
I'd never call the one I've fallen for "my ideology"
Like some young student or preacher in a church
Each morning I toss a coin to the shoeshine boy
And then go shooting up by elevator
To an awfully busy place, without women.

(*Cherry Tree in Leaf*, 1961)

HIROSHI SEKINE (1920–1994)

Leaving This Room

Leaving this room
The room that measured out my time

I carried out my books
I carried out my desk
I carried out my clothes
I carried out all sorts of junk
I carried out love, as well

The old-fashioned
Foot-warmer
The china brazier
I left behind
But what makes me sad
Is not that, of course:
It's the many memories I leave behind
That no moving van could bear away

In the now-empty room
All my memories are left behind
But I'll be back for them one day
For sure
Mr. Landlord!

(*The One Who Promised*, 1963)

A Single Strange Step

My kidney's run off to hospital so
Three times a week
Off I must go to meet it
It's bothersome but
When I think of those who go to work each day
I know I must put up with it

At first they couldn't get the dialytic needle in
It hurt a lot of times but
Thinking of those whose fated pain is worse
I shut my eyes
When at last I see again
So many others in their beds, their pillows side by side
I knew it was not time to feel
I bore the world's misfortune all alone

Some go back home
Refreshed as after the daily bath
Will I ever do the same?
I can't be born once more
But feel I've started life anew

(*A Single Strange Step*, 1989)

Shijimi Clams

I woke up in the middle of the night.
The shijimi clams I bought that evening
Were alive, mouths open
In a corner of the kitchen.

"When dawn comes
I'll eat you
Each and every one"

I gave an old hag's laugh.
After that
There was nothing left for me to do that night
But go to sleep
Mouth slightly open

(*Name-plates, Etc.*, 1968)

Name-plates

You must hang out the name-plate by yourself
On the place where you live.

Expect nothing
From a name-plate hung by another
On the place you sleep each night.

I went into hospital
And the name-plate said
"Miss Ishigaki Rin"—
They added the "Miss".

If I stop at an inn
There's no name on my door but
When they put me in the furnace of the crematorium
And shut that door
Above it they'll hang a plate that says
"Ms. Ishigaki Rin"
And how can I refuse?

"Miss"
"Ms."
I don't want them.

You must hang out the name-plate by yourself
On the place where you live.

And on the place where my spirit dwells
No one else must hang the name-plate
Ishigaki Rin
That will do.

(*Name-plates, Etc.*, 1968)

Land / Houses

They spread a sheet of paper
On one spot.

And built a house on top of "rights".

Time blew past like the wind
The globe rotated ceaselessly.

"Real Estate" has a nice ring,
"It's mine"
Sounds pretty good as well.

My neighbor with a smile
Gave the door a push and went on in.

That was it
A homely light was lit
Night deepened and the light went out.

The truly Real Thing
Had welcomed them.

How relieved they must have been.

(*Name-plates, Etc.*, 1968)

NOBUO AYUKAWA (1920–1986)

A Morning Song at the Moored Boat Hotel

Through the rain that had begun to pour down
You tried simply to go someplace far away
Looking for an overpass to death
You tried to distance yourself from the city of sorrow
When I held your wetted shoulder with my arm
The raw night-wind city
Seemed to me like a port
Lighting each and every cabin's lamp
With the sweet nostalgia of the soul,
A huge black shadow crouched upon the wharf
Let's throw off dripping-wet regrets
And go upon a voyage
Carrying you like a rucksack over my shoulder
Let's go upon a voyage, I thought
The faint moaning of the electric lines
Seemed like a ringing in the ears flying across the sea

In our dawn
A speeding ship of steel
Was to have borne our destinies amid the blue sea waters
And yet we
Never went anywhere
From the window of our cheap hotel
I spat toward the town at dawn
My heavy weary eyelids
Drooped like an ashen wall
The vain hopes and dreams of you and me
Were bottled up in a glass vase
The end of the broken-down quay
Was dissolving in the foul water of the vase
Insufficient sleep somehow
Stagnated there like a bad-odored medicine

But yesterday's rain
Endlessly kept falling on the empty melancholy valley
Between our hearts, torn apart, and
Our warm, flushed flesh

Have we strangled our god to death in our bed?
You're thinking it's my responsibility
I'm thinking it's yours
I put on my chronic gastro-enteric patient's sloppy tie
You make up your little face, vulture-like above sagging shoulders
And we sit at the breakfast table
Facing a future half-formed
Within the cracked egg
You show a foolish, riddling smile
I make a stab with the fork of hatred
Looking as if I'd eaten a whole oily plateful
Of bourgeois adultery

The view from the window
Is set within a frame
Ah, I long for rain and city-streets and night
Until night comes
I cannot well embrace
The scene of this city of fatigue
Born between the two Great Wars of West and East
A failure in love and revolution both
From the window appears that ideologue's scowling face
He who suddenly turned and plunged to the depths
The streets are dead
The fresh morning breeze
Places against my neck, rubbed raw by its metal collar,
A cool razor blade
The figure standing next to the canal
Seems to me a wolf that,
Its heart removed,
Will never howl again

(*The Person on the Bridge*, 1963)

Heaven

Against the frozen night sky of November
He stood, shoulders hunched
On the almost empty train platform
A pale young girl
Was talking with another
    Someplace, they say,
      There was a place called Heaven
      A place of dazzling light

Against the frozen night sky of November
A single little star twinkled
Like the young girl
He had to return to someplace too
Someplace
Dark and cold

    And, they say, there was a very pretty field of flowers
    There
As if she were walking through a distant town
The girl's memories
Seemed to break off, and then go on again
Against the frozen night sky of November
The advertising lights went out
The cold wind, a thin-bladed knife
Cut through the rough skin of the city

12:10   The eye of the needle
Peers intently into the heart's darkness
There, with soup gone cold before her
A woman waits for his return
Her face unmoving
There
A simple wooden bed
Unmoving

And there, they say,
A man called God was living
Then, what happened after that?
The voice just stopped
Against the frozen night sky of November
Scared of happiness unseen
The two girls drew their shadowy wings together
The sound of the last train upon the rails
Ran through a distant land
Forever

(*The Poems of Nobuo Ayukawa, 1945–1955*, 1955)

If Now You Suffer

The day's work over
About to sleep
You must forgive everyone
    You can forgive
    Even those who kill you
Forgiving
Is the privilege of all
Those who don't forgive
Are not forgiven
That is the way of this world
But one cannot judge oneself so
You cannot forgive yourself
That is the rule
Just to live
And to live long, all the more
Provides a boundless store of reasons
Not to forgive oneself
    If by good chance
    Someone comes to kill you
    Greet him with joy
Permitting oneself to forgive
Is all that's left to us
To ease our heavy burden

(*Shukurenkō*, 1978)

TOYOICHIRŌ MIYOSHI (1920–1992)

Prisoner

Waking up at midnight, no one's there —
The dog, startled, suddenly begins to howl
Trying to leap up to the height of every slumber
All ears are in the bed
The bed is in the clouds

Terrified of loneliness, the dog clashes its teeth
Leaping up, then slipping and falling, the voice of despair
Each time I slip a little from the bed

My eyes, two holes dug into a wall
Dreams sit frozen on the desk like phosphorescence
In the heavens a redly blazing star
On the earth a sadly howling dog
    (From somewhere a faint echo comes back)
I know the secret:
Closed up inside the prison of my heart a dog is howling
The sleepless pallid dog of "Vie"

(Prisoner, 1949)

Our Song of a May Night

The earth is supported   by a thousand hands, by a thousand
        pains
The earth is held captive   by ten thousand hands, by ten
        thousand anxieties
The earth is enclosed   by one hundred million hands, by one
        hundred million fears
The earth is suspended   above a struggle with want and
        barrenness and ruin

Our ears sleep in the mire
Our eyes wake in the night
Our hair is tousled in the wind
The wind blows over the stones where we sleep
An Eldorado upon the stones
An olive tree among the ruins
The yellow nails of the gravedigger —
In the mirror
She sleeps among the withered leaves of eternity
        heaped up beneath the waters
Desire is a restless fish swimming in the spaces between
        imprisoned dreams

The trees are sobbing
She is calling, from far away
I am replying, from here
The wind silences it all with its loud voice
She hides at her breast a small salt-cellar
I have in a large cup bitter wine
Into her salt-cellar   I pour one drop of wine
It is a crystal of rapture   a bracelet of love
It becomes a lovely flower
        releasing its mellow scent in the dark night
We embrace each other and sleep in the sunken, ashen-colored
        privates of the earth

The summer horizon is ablaze with scarlet
It is the season of hunger and thirst and weariness and decay
We have no hometown to return to
The Orient, a living victim in search of shade in a sea of sand
Old armor and helmets   and two lovers
We've lost a friend
A merry mountain sparrow pursued above the brutal abyss
A pallid head thrust out toward the future   and so many of
    that ilk
An indestructible cross, the striped pattern of blind fate
    tattooed upon his forehead
And, if something else is left,
It would be a confidence in destruction
A faith in resurrection

Our throats seek a clear, pure spring
Our hands stroke the fresh night skies of May
We each of us sleep embracing our own worlds
Our own hopeful futures
The wind blows across our dreams
A rainbow bridge of sorrow suspended in the void
They rule the earth   rule the sun   rule our hopes
    those heavy wings of the bird of night
Death is greater even than our illusions
Silence is deeper even than the sea...

(*Poems of Toyoichirō Miyoshi*, 1970)

TARŌ NAKA (1922–)

Tower

In delicate darkness, drifting darkness
My digits dream
The sere sensation of weeping willows
The waxing warmth of double trembling doves
Dampens my palm
The eyes of the doves
    But in the darkness
    The unseen eyes see
    A faded fortress
    A transparent tower

In the bright-pink haze, the blazing haze
My dreaming digits
Reaching reverie, softly sweet stretching skin
Lingering at the limits of lonely sand-dunes
From a growth of gromwells
The smell of salt-water swelling over
The sadness of a shell wailing in the waves
On the beach by my back-of-beyond village
    But within the haze
    Seen by the unseen eyes
    A closed-up castle
    A too-distant tower

Drifting darkness, blazing haze
Fingers fumbling
In reverie, the lifeline of the cold crag
Impassioned panting
Silvery spray
    But
    In the unseen eyes
    A closed-mouthed castle
    An untouchable tower...

(Music, 1965)

The Sea of Sleep

The sky, a darkly tilting sea
The sea, a limitless gray wall
The wall, the weight of smoky thought of lassitude
Bearing up under that weight
Swim, swim, swim
Groaning, roiling, moaning, squirming, the sea's sadness
Stretching far, wave upon wave
The limitless weight
Through the gray weight
Swimming, swimming to the offing, to the offing
Of fearful thoughts
Drunken dissolves in the night fog
Drifting dreams in the darkness of distorted nights
Through the night
Forlornly
Toward the dawn
Through the darkness of infinite emptiness
Upon onrushing wave after onrushing wave
Alone
Toward the faint gleam of porcelain skin
Stretching, scratching, shrinking, dragging
Kick, kick, kick, stiffen, kick
Sheets of Nothingness entangle the body
The non-existent Now
The vain waves
The heart's sea
Within that dark sea
The roar of time
The sliding of the waves
A distant lighthouse
A meager light
Suddenly I vomit violently
From my empty belly
From my dry throat
An opaque jellyfish
Of distant memories of muddy sludge
The empty corpses of blind men

Whose songs about the coiling time are lost
I vomit them violently, vomit without stopping
Leaden smoke of distant battles
Pond scum
Sex of animals' sleep
Bronze wordless voices
Tangles of hair
Sorrowful windings of a snake
A life of anger's blood
I vomit it all out violently
Not a transparent bird
Not a green bird
A black-blood bird
A blazing bird, a scorched-black bird
From my dry-as-dust throat
A bird takes flight
Aah —
In that voiceless cry
I drown
The pallid porcelain sky
Tore apart
And began to drip graceful filaments of steel

(*Music*, 1965)

TAKAYUKI KIYO'OKA (1922–2006)

Alabaster

A nude statue so white it seemed frozen
Suspended in my dream

The chisel marks that shaped it
Blown about by the winds of my dream

My sorrow-filled eyes
Knew that face from somewhere

Ah
How strange it seems that you should have a body

★

On your color-blind red lips
The sound first hesitates

Over your idiot-clear eyes
A shadow first passes

In a limitless distant time
A bell tolls, telling of your birth

The inside of your frozen alabaster knee shows
The struggles of the murmuring band of death

★

Are you ashamed
Of the chill arrogance secretly rising there?

Will I regret when
Time begins to alter your appearance?

A kiss within the eye of the oncoming typhoon
Or perhaps within one sharp clear glance
Of our crystallized despair

★

A flood of blood that breaks the alabaster skin
Piercing the mirror with the point of a pin   the refreshing smell
    of corruption

The cycle of flames marring the alabaster symmetry
Licking off the stars with a bestial tongue   those pure dark tears

In the round-dance of the murmuring band of death
Uniting you and the universe with me –
That first   and   limitless night

(Frozen Flames, 1959)

Through the Ear

When your heart is impoverished, don't listen to music.
Go and eat silence
Where there is only air and water and stones!
From far off will come an echo of
The words you need to live.

(Sketches of the Four Seasons, 1966)

An Ecstasy of Sloth

He doesn't shave his gleaming whiskers
Or cut his shining hair
He disconnects the grape-shaped bell there in the
    entrance-way.
He doesn't answer the phone when it rings too early.
He doesn't open the mail that comes through the door-slot
    as if by right.
The laundry's left hanging to dry inside his room
So who needs a light set of drawers?
Money's been dropped in every corner of the house
So who needs a heavy wallet?
But even though he's forgotten what it is to clean
Obsessed instead with his globe of the world
He has to eat and drink a bit.
He needs a little clean air and sunlight.
Oh,
And yeah, he wants to play a little ball.
Wants to take a bath to music.
At the end of a sleep as long as the equator
He vaguely saw
A distant dream
Of a beauteous woman bestriding a castle in the clouds.

(Firm Buds, 1975)

TARŌ KITAMURA (1922–1992)

Rain

Spring reflects in every heavy window the image of the town.
In the town the rain never stops falling,
The place to which our deaths will someday come is misted over.
The common graveyard atop the hill.
The graves burn crosses deep within the eyes of every one of us,
Trying to measure all our pleasures.
The rain blurs the little town with its geranium plants
Between the graveyard and the window.
The sound of turning wheels vanishes in the quiet rain
The rain vanishes in the screeching of the wheels.
We gaze at the graveyard
Seeking beneath the stones the hoarse call of death.
Everything is there,
Every joy and sorrow at once binds us to that place.
The common graveyard atop the hill.
From the bread factory made of brick
A burnt smell comes, as if to mock us,
Filling the streets with quiet illusion.
What does illusion give us?
How
Why are we such hollow existences?
The blond stream beneath the bridge
All flows
In our innards death flows.
Eleven a.m.
The rain, in the screeching of the wheels,
The sound of turning wheels vanishes in the quiet rain.
In the town the rain never stops falling
Staying behind the heavy glass
We move our hands and feet as we lie there.

(*The Poems of Tarō Kitamura, 1947–1966*, 1966)

Morning Mirror

A drop of morning water
Gleams upon the narrow razor blade and
Falls — Is that
One's life? How strange.
Why do I go on living?
With eyes that seem to gaze the livelong day
At the ocean beneath a cloudy sky,
I've passed over half my life.

"To become a corpse —
That should always be the image of one's life.
One must count upon a hideous death
And await the approaching hour."
That was once my consolation.
Ah, a thought as dry as wafers in the mouth!

Pride and vanity! My
Little empire's gone. Yet no one
Punished me. Quite
Wrong though I was! Africa's
Dreadful scenes spread out white
Against the strong, strong light. And

Still I see in the window that same view. (Good morning,
Woman! Fragrance of gardenias!) A positive view of life
As futile as the ashes of some cigar. Good morning,
O stench of death! O cheerful hard-working men!
I brush my teeth, and carefully, with soap,
Wash my hands and look into the mirror.

A drop of morning water
Gleams upon the narrow razor blade and
Falls — Is that
One's life? How cruel.

Why do I go on living?
With eyes that seem to gaze the livelong day
At the stormy ocean,
I've passed over half my life.

(*The Poems of Tarō Kitamura, 1947–1966*, 1966)

Sinking Temple

People all over the world are looking for proof of death   But
no one, no not one, has seen death   People are finally no more
than illusions
Reality, perhaps, is the greatest common measure of such things
In place of people all things begin to ask questions   about life
about its existence
It may have all begun from a single chair, yet I am filled with fear
Reality, perhaps, is the least common multiple of such things   By
the by, how is it   that those who cannot feel sadness at man's
fate could stake their very selves on this world of strife? At times
persons of genius have appeared but they did no more than make
the nothingness all the more subtle   That which is self-evident
has only deepened the vortex of broad daylight

He may have been trying to tell us something   But I shall write
only of the facts   First he fell to the ground as if breaking at the
knees   Among those who ran to him a youth of about my age
murmured to himself the words "A beautiful face   And, more's
the pity, he believes the world to be a kind of flower!"

(*Four Thousand Days and Nights*, 1956)

Etching

A view from a German etching he had seen   now appears before his
  eyes
It seems to be a bird's-eye view of an ancient city moving from twilight
  into night
Or it might have been a realistic copy of the precipice of modernity
  being led from the dead of night into the dawn

This man   whom I have spoken of as "he"   when young killed his
  father
That autumn his mother beautifully went mad

(Four Thousand Days and Nights, 1956)

The Gods of Poetry

Mokichi's god of poesy
Was the Kannon at Asakusa, and sweet broiled eel

"Form" was his rampart:
He had only to go to Asakusa's Thunder Gate

My neurotic deity
Is always in the worst of moods
Doesn't even bother to buy fire insurance

A small house and
A big silence

(A New Year's Letter, 1973)

TAKA'AKI YOSHIMOTO (1924–)

Descent to a Singular World

Descending to a singular world he feels
Regret
That he didn't share the little secrets of his life
With the girl in the world he's left behind
That he did not know the pleasures of seeing
The remaining fragments of desire
Change into the fine rich smell of fresh-baked bread
And the self-effacing bows of other men

And yet
The parting of the ways between one world and the other
Was quite simple   A dark spirit
Faced the rulers above the burnt and suppurating
Ruins of the capital
Saying "I don't want to, I won't!"
A ragged child of war deftly stole his wallet
At the same moment his world too was stolen away

Neither the wind that passes as if through a net
Between buildings erected as if at random
Nor the cheerful girl in the midst of a happy-looking crowd
Can play upon his heart
Caresses pouring down like rain upon his living flesh
Cannot decide his spirit
When he's lost any reason to live
He lives   When close to death
He seeks, but cannot find, a reason to die
His heart
Had already descended to the singular world
His flesh for ten more years
Walked among the gaudy throng

Surrounded by secrets
His heart filled with dreams perhaps unrealizable
Love affairs, hungry, unsupported
Vanishing love
Ashamed of what is written down on paper
He sets out for the future

(*The Complete Works of Taka'aki Yoshimoto, Vol. 1 Poetry*, 1968)

At Tsukuda Ferry

At Tsukuda Ferry my daughter said
"The water's clean   like the seashore we went to in summer"
Not at all   Take a look
Near the stern of the river steamer tied there
You can see garbage build-up, swayed by the river
It's always been that way
(From now on I'll speak to my heart so my daughter will not hear)
The water is dark and rather stagnant   beneath a chill and rainy sky
Its twisting and turning like a large sewer is a sign the river is old
Among the convoluted canals upon the island in the river
Was the town where I lived
Crabs too could still live there then and
I went to catch some
My feet stepped into the mud and I began to swim
At Tsukuda Ferry my daughter said
"What bird is that?"
"A seagull"
"No, the black one over there!"
It must be a black kite
They were here in the old days too
It flew among its seagull companions
To pick at rats' corpses and fish innards floating by
(From here on I'll speak to my heart so my daughter will not hear)
To live surrounded by water
Has always something of a fortress-feel

In my dreams the canals' flowing waters always appear
Why the bridges? So the boy leaning out with his hands upon the rail
Could, if he had some sorrow,
Let it float away

"That's Sumiyoshi Shrine
Where they have the Tsukuda Festival
That's the primary school   See how small it is"
I can say no more to my daughter
The old town now looks small
As if to fit within the hollow between the lines of feeling, intellect,
    and life within one's palm
All distances look small
The same with our philosophies
The old far-distances have shrunk
Along the streets where once I lived
Taking my daughter's hand   wet by the chill rain
I rush on by

(*The Replica and the Mirror*, 1964)

I Was Born

It must have been shortly after I started to learn English.

A summer twilight. As I was walking through the temple grounds with my father, a pale woman came toward us, as if floating up from the blue depths of the evening haze. Slowly, languidly.

The woman seemed to be with child. I felt constrained by my father's presence, but did not shift my gaze from her stomach. Imagining the child headfirst in her womb and gently squirming, how strange it seemed that it would soon be born into this world.

The woman passed.

A boy's thoughts tend to leap. I understood in that instant that *to be born* is truly something *passive*. Excited, I addressed my father.
— "I was born" — that's what they say in English!
My father looked doubtfully into my face. I repeated:
— "I was born." It's in passive voice! Humans are caused to be born, is what we should say. It's not our own free act —
How surprised my father must have been to hear these words from his son. Could the look on my face have seemed merely innocent in his eyes? I was far too young to understand. To me it was just a simple grammatical discovery.

My father walked in silence for a while and then said an unexpected thing.
— There are dayflies that live just two or three days, then die. So why are they born at all, I used to wonder; it bothered me a lot.
I looked at my father. He went on.
— I asked a friend one day, and he showed me a female dayfly through a magnifying glass. He said its mouth was so recessed it couldn't really eat. Open its belly and there'd be nothing but air. And that's the way it was. But there were eggs, lots of them, right up into its narrow chest. It was like the misery of living and dying

dizzyingly repeated had choked it right up its throat. Cold, shining beads, they seemed. "The eggs," I said, turning toward my friend. He nodded: "Painful, isn't it?" And it was only a little while later that your mother had you, then passed away right after —

I no longer remember what my father went on to say. But there was one thing that stayed burned into my brain, painfully, pitifully.
— Blocking and choking my mother, even to her narrow chest: my pale body.

(News, 1957)

Evening Afterglow

The usual thing:
The train was full.
And
The usual thing:
Young people were seated,
Old persons stood.
A girl who'd sat with her head bent
Stood and gave her seat to someone old,
Who hurried to sit down.
At the next stop off he got without a word of thanks.
The girl sat down.
Another elder stood before her
Pushed there by the crowd.
The girl bent her head.
But
Standing once again
She gave her seat
To the old man.
At the next stop off he got, but with a word of thanks.
The girl sat down.
"What happens twice...," the saying goes:
Another elder stood before her
Pushed there by the crowd.
Poor thing

The girl bent her head
And this time did not stand.
The next station came
And then the next.
She bit her lower lip
Her body stiffened –
I got off the train.
Tense, with head bent,
How far did she go, I wonder,
That young girl?
The gentle of heart
In every time and place
Suffer, willy-nilly.
And why?
Because the gentle of heart
Feel
The pain of others as their own.
How far can she go, I wonder,
That young girl
Reproached by her gentle heart,
Biting her lower lip,
Pained,
Not looking at the lovely evening afterglow?

(*Illusion, Method*, 1959)

Epithalamium

To live closely together
It's best to be a little foolish
Not too grand
It's best to be aware that
Nothing too grand
Lasts long
It's best not to seek perfection
"Perfection is unnatural"
It's best to say with nonchalance
It's best if one of you
Likes a joke
Likes to fool around
If you criticize each other
It's best to wonder
Later
Whether you had the right to criticize
When you speak the truth
It's best to hold back a little
When you speak the truth
It's best to be aware
How easily the other may be hurt
Don't be too eager
For the stress and strain of trying
To be too grand
To be too right
It's best to be bathed in light
Calmly, in full measure
To be healthy, and even when winds blow
Just moved, and grateful to be alive
There should be days like that
And
Though nothing is said
I want you both to know
Why your hearts are moved

(*When the Wind Blows*, 1977)

NORIKO IBARAGI (1926–2006)

When I Was at My Prettiest

When I was at my prettiest
The streets were ruined and empty
And the blue sky could be glimpsed
From places quite absurd

When I was at my prettiest
A lot of those around me died
In factories, at sea, on nameless islands
I missed my chance to wear nice clothes

When I was at my prettiest
No one gave me lovely gifts
The men knew only to salute
They all went off and left behind
Only their winning glances

When I was at my prettiest
My head was empty
My heart was hard as stone
Only my arms and legs shone chestnut-colored

When I was at my prettiest
My country lost the war
Ah, what could be more stupid!
With blouse sleeves rolled
I strutted the mean streets

When I was at my prettiest
Jazz spilled from all the radios
Feeling as dizzy as when I smoked my first cigarette
I gorged on the sweet music of a foreign land

When I was at my prettiest
I was so very unhappy
I was so very foolish
I was so awfully lonely

And so I decided to live as long as ever I could
Like that Rouault of France
Who made such beautiful paintings
After he'd grown old

(*Invisible Deliveryman*, 1958)

It's Your Own Sensibility

When your heart becomes dry as dust
Don't blame it on others
Having neglected to water it yourself

When you've turned into a difficult tiresome person
Don't blame your friends
Who's the one who has lost all grace?

When you're filled with irritation
Don't blame your relations
You were the one who was inept at everything

When your "beginner's mind" has begun to disappear
Don't blame your daily life
Your resolution was too frail to begin with

For everything that's wrong
Don't blame the times
That would be to cast aside your slightly radiant dignity

It's your own sensibility
Guard it yourself
You fool

(It's Your Own Sensibility, 1977)

A Tree's Fruit

On a twig high up
One large green piece of fruit
A local youth climbed right up
Stretched out a hand to reach it, slipped and fell
What had seemed to be a piece of fruit
Was a moss-covered skull

Mindanao
Twenty-six years
The tiny branch of a jungle tree
Had somehow snagged the skull of
A Japanese soldier, dead in the war
Was it an eye-socket or a nostril-hole?
Unaware, the twig grew and grew into
A strong young tree

In life
There must have been a woman who clasped to her breast
This head
As something beloved and precious

What mother steadily gazed
At this small temple's pulse?
What woman twined this hair around her fingers
Gently drawing him nearer?
Had it   been   me...

I broke off there   and let a year's weeks and months flow by
Then took the poem from the drawer
I could not find   the final line
More years   went by

Had it   been   me...
The line that follows   will not come

(*It's Your Own Sensibility*, 1977)

MINORU NAKAMURA (1927–)

Night

Did the suffocating days flow away, like a doe in flight, I wonder…
On lonely nights I waited   among the odors of rotting seaweed
Among seething thoughts of metallic sake – how many nights have
    been submerged, I wonder…

There was something that drew near the folds of the waves   It
    seemed to call without a voice
The dark sea rocked   women's necks, blue from strangulation,
And a vermilion staircase, broken…
The water trembled slightly   There was a rough and bestial hand

How many tombs did the submerged nights seek, I wonder…
Have they forgotten the numberless downcast eyes, I wonder…
The dark sea rocked   women's necks, blue from strangulation
And a vermilion staircase, broken…

The nights will pass like flaming feathered arrows
They will hide themselves as they seek their tombs in the depths of
    the sea…
In the folds of the waves was a large and bestial hand that
    imprisoned my lonely nights

(*Songs without Words*, 1950)

The Kite

The dawn sky was dry in the blowing wind
The wind blew against it, but the kite did not move
It was not that it didn't move at all   High in the sky
It tried continually to dance higher

In truth it was continually dancing
Tied to the earth by a narrow cord
Resisting the wind, riding the wind
It worked carefully to preserve its balance

O there was in the depths of my memory a sinking swamp
And a city utterly destroyed   People crushed in despair
And the sky above, quite dry...

The wind blew against it, but the kite did not move
It wasn't that it didn't move at all   But high up in the sky
The sound of its humming was very hard to hear...

(*Trees*, 1954)

TAKASHI TSUJII (1927–)

The White Horse

In the hour of change from day to night   that always comes
When stillness falls upon the town
And the flow of cars breaks off
I see him
A white horse   at last
Slowly leaving

Elegantly
He lifts his head, near wistfully
His mane flowing to left and right
He stops   and paws the hardened pavement
With soft hooves
As if trying to remember something

Then   the windows of the buildings are eyeless sockets
The avenue of trees has prepared a funeral ode
They bend the knee, my white horse, my career
What lifts its head
Heart vanished far away
Is my betrayal of him, and his of me

When I was a boy still seeking the unknown
The white horse would always stand upon a wild mountain top
Following the valleys   blown by the wind
Sometimes racing to answer my whistle
He turned toward me   pawing the dew-laden grass
When, then, did he begin to wander the city streets?

My white horse
Seems to have forgotten his own words
The city streets do not speak to him
The sound of one falling into hell
Echoes to the soft rhythm of horseshoes
Always he eats only lemons

Or could it be the city in itself
That's wandering?
In winter   the clouds of summer rise
Tanks pass along a road just by the sea
Last year was a strange one but
Everyone seems to have forgotten the white horse
What with demonstrations, gorgeous weddings, nuclear blasts

In such a season
When a net of silence covers all
Those who have a native place think back to it
Those who have a house and family feel concerned
Only those who have nothing at all
Trying to see themselves
Discover the white horse
Their dusty   starving horse

And yet
In an atmosphere thick with mackerel oil
What could it be that loudly cracks its whip over my heart
And keeps on running?
An ancient city presumed long dead
Or
A fairy tale, perhaps, presumed forgotten?

I want someone   to tell me, please
In a momentary stillness
When no trees speak to me   no rays of sunlight fall
In the hour when the scent of lemons alone
Crawls ghost-like upon the buildings' walls
The white horse's pedigree and place of origin
And where my fabled horse might have gone

(*Poems of Takashi Tsujii*, 1967)

RYŪSEI HASEGAWA (1928–)

The Laborer's Eyes

When the laborer was working in the park
Covering her face with an umbrella
A woman went by
The laborer stopped his digging   and checked the time
He watched her retreating figure until it disappeared

When the laborer was working in the park
A young man and   a pale pregnant woman
Stopped for a while to gaze at a bare transplanted tree
The laborer lit a cigarette with his gloved hands
Grinning he called to his coworker at the bottom of the hole

When the laborer was working in the park
An old man who lived alone tottered by
The laborer looked up at the varicose-veined and spotted legs
Stray sounds drifted by
A piece from the Noh play *Aridōshi*   or a Tendai
    Buddhist liturgical chant?

When the laborer was working in the park
Two persons with long hair, male or female, who could tell?
Went by   entangled with each other
The laborer spat hard
And pitched the dirt high against the blue sky

When   will the park   be finished?
Right by the work-place   dogs pass and humans too
The laborer's eyes are keenly open to the world
Noting   on what day   at what hour   who passed
Where they came from and how they went their way

The sun sets   and the laborer goes home
I watch   his retreating figure
The eyes   These eyes are the only things worth trusting
I want to work!

(*The Poetic Life*, 1978)

ERIKO KISHIDA (1929–)

The Soundless Girl

There was a clever boy. When he'd leave off whistling, he would examine the far distance with a pair of binoculars. When he grew tired of the binoculars, he would play with a tape-recorder. Or, at times he would examine a girl with his binoculars and record the sounds she made on the tape-recorder, as he whistled the tune "I Love Your Eyes." Her mind was more tender than he'd expected, and seemed to ripple. Her lips were unopened buds, so nothing ask! And her ears—ah, there was no sound. The clever boy took notes.

One day there was a strange girl there. Let me explain in what way she was strange. Her footsteps were the road's footsteps, the sound of her running was the sound of the wind running. So when the girl ate an apricot, there was the sound of the apricot eating her. When the girl swam, the sea came for a swim. The boy wondered, then, which was real? Which sound he should tape-record? What if the girl should like me? The boy was suddenly afraid. The boy by then already liked the girl. I think you know what comes next. The boy stopped taking notes. He put his ear to the girl's ear. And—ah, there was a sound. This ear—ah, it's my sound, my sound! the boy said.

(*Lion Stories*, 1957)

Why Do Flowers Always

Why   do flowers always
Take the form of replies?
Why   do only questions
Rain down   from the sky?

(*Songs on a Bright Day*, 1979)

KAZUE SHINKAWA (1929–)

Don't Bunch Me

Don't bunch me
Like gillyflowers
Like white leeks
Don't bunch me please   I'm ears of rice
In autumn   when the earth scorches its breast
As far as the eye can see golden-colored ears of rice

Don't fix me in place
Like an insect in a specimen case
Like a picture postcard from some highlands
Don't fix me in place please   I'm the flutter of wings
Constantly exploring the breadth of the sky
The sound of invisible wings

Don't pour me out
Like milk thinned with everydayness
Like half-warmed sake
Don't pour me out please   I'm the ocean
At night   impossibly full
A bitter tide   boundless waters

Don't name me
With the name of daughter   the name of wife
Don't make me stay in place please
Under the heavy name of mother   I'm the wind
The wind that knows where the spring   and the apple tree
Are to be found

Don't segment me
With periods and commas and several neat paragraphs
And, like a letter with "Farewell" at the end
Don't bring me to a brisk conclusion please   I'm writing
   that has no end
Like a river
Endlessly flowing   spreading   a poem in one line

(*Not Metaphor*, 1968)

Song

When a woman has her first child
The song that slips of itself
From her lips
Is the gentlest song in the world
From afar
It softly calms the rough and bristling
Mane of the sea
It makes the stars nod their heads
Makes the traveler look back
In a lonely valley forgotten even by the wind
It lights red lamps
Upon the thin branches of an apple tree
Oh, if it were not so
How could she raise her child?
This lovely
Defenseless one

(*13 Odes to the Earth*, 1974)

Swan

Your wings will get wet, O swan
As I gaze at them
They seem about to shatter
Faintly, the sound of wings

In dreams you will be wetted, O swan
In whose dreams are you being seen?

Filling, then trickling down
Their light streams into your wings
The various stars that speak to you

When shadows are reflected in a blue sky
Do they become white?

From birth you've known the secret
A swan will finally
In a pattern of light
Colored by the fragrant morning sunlight
Go toward the sky

A form has already been given you
For bashfulness   white swan
Almost about
To take on color

O swan

(Swan, 1955)

Wedding March

A penetrating
Smell of fruits mingles in the breeze, yes
The bride's veil seems
Softly
Slightly to move, yes
In a forest an animal
Swivels its head around
Trying to lick its back, yes
On and on they go
The congratulatory speeches, yes
An uncle steals a glance at the bride's nape, yes
The groom's Section Chief
Finishes his well-made speech
Working in advertisements for the company products, yes
Only frogs, lizards, and foxes are truly monogamous, yes
Tapeworms have intercourse with themselves
Using the male and female organs in each segment of their bodies
All their lives, yes
The bride suddenly remembers her lover's mouth, how it looked
    both cool and hot, yes
The groom remembers his national pension plan number, yes
In a river a crocodile bares its white belly to the blue sky, yes
A branch breaks and at once
A pleasant smell spreads over the river's surface, yes
In town shoes are selling well, yes
On and on they go
The congratulatory speeches, yes
Words of farewell to the new bride and groom, yes
A husband should praise his wife's cooking
And occasionally bring her flowers, yes
O, buy her a whole boatload of giant flowers from some southern
    island, yes
A man's got to spend a lot of time with bosses and coworkers, yes

The aunt who served as go-between suddenly looks down, yes
Good things, then bad things
And after the bad things, good things again, yes
When it clears, the stars appear, yes
On and on they go
The plagiarized words of congratulation, yes
At the request of both families
Sending off the new couple on their honeymoon trip
Is gratefully declined
O, who would want to send them off, yes
Keep the honeymoon trip a secret, yes
We're charmed by
All we do not understand, yes
On an ocean the waves move toward the horizon
Trying to bury the sky above in waves, yes
The groom had better buy some swimming trunks, yes
You'll get a sudden urge to go to the ocean, yes
It's going to be tough from now on, yes
Time on your own
Gone forever, yes
She'd stab away at a dead chicken, "the little woman," yes
You're on your own now, yes

(*How Trees Think*, 1964)

Walls of Lead

Words
They would rather not have been born as words
They think, in words
They would rather have been born as towering walls of lead
They think
And
Later
They give a single, wordless sigh

(*Poems of Hiroshi Kawasaki*, 1968)

KŌICHI IIJIMA (1930–)

Understanding

"To live is to share—" Paul Éluard

People look at each other as if they were animals made from bread.
They have nothing to share, it seems.
A man walks on tossing out one by one
The things he has stuffed in his pockets.
Whether they are stones
Or slips of paper with writing on them
He finds no one who will take them.

Could this be my old familiar earthly friend?
Could these be page after page of the thick book called life,
Remembered all the more fondly with the passage of the years
After the body has died?
Even while hating that we do not understand one another
    we remain stubbornly silent.
Not understanding one single thing
    we make our selves invisible.

(*Another's Sky*, 1971)

Mother Tongue

For the half year I was abroad
I never once thought
Of writing poems
I forgot myself
As I walked about
Asked why I wrote no poems
I never could reply.

I returned to Japan
And soon
I could not help writing poems
Now at last I understand
How I could go along for that half year
Without writing poems.
I have returned to the language of my motherland again.

Mother and land and language
For the half year when I told myself I was cut off from
Mother and land and language
I walked uninjured
Through reality.
There was little need
To write poems.

In April Paul Celan
Drowned himself in the River Seine, and
That act by this poet who was a Jew
Is comprehensible to me.
Poetry is full of sorrows
Poetry, they say, corrects the nation's tongue
But not for me
Day by day I am wounded in my mother tongue
Each night   I must set forth
Toward another mother tongue
That makes me write poems   and lets me go on living.

(*What Was Goya's First Name?*, 1974)

The Roads of Miyakojima

Human beings live in houses
I felt strongly
The first time I went to Karimata and Ikema
I walked along
Feeling two eyes
Peek out at me every so often
From behind the curtains and wooden doors
I walked along the winding roads
Almost shuddering
The narrow roads
Ran through every village
In the same ancient curves
Here and there was a shop
With no name
The twists and turns of those roads entered my body
They are part of my body now
The roads, the roads, I mutter
As I push my way through underground passages
Filled with milling crowds.

(*Miyako*, 1979)

CHIMAKO TADA (1930–2003)

First Dream of the New Year

Listening to the last tolling of the bells on New Year's Eve
I started to peel a tangerine's golden skin
An old man, pushing back against my fingers, stuck his head out
    from where the skin was torn
    — Oh, do come in   It's warm inside
(But how could I go inside?)
Peeking into the hole I was sucked in headfirst
And found myself seated inside the tangerine
The walls of the round room were covered in something soft and
    white
And indeed, it was "warm inside"
In front of the old man stood a Go board
It seemed he'd wanted someone to play against
I chose black and he beat me easily
Then beamed and handed me a tangerine from his bowl
As I started to peel its fragrant skin
Yet another old man stuck out his head
— Oh, do come in
In how many round rooms
And tangerines within tangerines
Did I enjoy myself?
When I awoke to the first light of New Year's Day
My body was steeped in the scent of dazzling gold

(Festival Bonfire, 1986)

TAKASUKE SHIBUSAWA (1930–1998)

A Crystal Madness

At last it's a crystal madness
Running through both death and love alike
What kind of transparent madness
Is trying to live the coming crystal
A painful gleam
One scream now slides down and enters into nothingness
Nothingness is a cage made by his impotence
Flowers on a crag   quiet madness
One scream now is changing
The places near the ice-grass, whose name has never yet been
    spoken
Into the flesh of births and encounters.
If madness too has its logic
There should be no
Flowers on a crag   quiet madness
And finally no zero
Only a gathered crystal stare   shining in the depths
This metaphoric spiral nebula
Both formerly and now at a terrifyingly clear speed
Circling fever   chaos   the depths of the earth
And denying them – Is that an encounter?
That a birth?
O sharp precipice!
The sudden leaning   and the disarmed sky
At the lonely promontory where the mirror's spell was broken
The risen phantom-sun
Violently rapes the crags here and there
The many crystals change their form of crystallization   at last
That's how it seems to me   because
Just as there is no one who can rob me of the ties that bind to
    one who died too young,
So there is no one who can deny the meaning of the as-yet-unborn
    words

That wail in this dark abyss of here and now
A painful gleam   flowers on a crag   and
A clear and quiet madness
Running through both death and love alike
At the critical angle of the reticulated world that is now coming
It is a clear and quiet madness   a crystal madness

(*Lacquer or Crystal Madness*, 1969)

Ode on Passing through Winter

At the very limits of intoxication
Toward what did he awaken?
That time of frenzied degradation and loss of Nature's
    radiance crept closer
As the man who had left the act of writing far behind
Asked himself if for him
Compassion might not be brother to death
That man who went far beyond the act of writing
And on the other hand
There was one who brought down
The light of hopeful stars onto the darkness of books
As he elaborated secret stratagems for
Using the heat of festivals in mountain valleys
To melt the frozen tribal words that echoed in the winter cold
With the heat of festivals in mountain valleys
At the very limits of awakening
Toward what did he grow drunk?
Cold paintings and the desert wind
Yielding to this place yet with nowhere truly to live
Whose voice commands me
O hang your head!
Worship that which you have burned
And burn that which you have worshipped

(*Ode on Passing through Winter*, 1977)

MAKOTO ŌOKA (1931–)

For Spring

Digging up the springtime spent drowsing on the sandy beach
You use it to adorn your hair   You laugh
The foam of your laughter scattering like ripples in the sky
The sea quietly warms the grass–green sun

Your hand in mine
Your stone tossed against my sky   ah
The shades of flower petals flowing beneath today's sky

New buds emerging in our arms
At the center of our field of vision
A golden sun rotates, spray rising
We   are lakes, are trees
Are the rays of sunlight dappling the lawn beneath the trees
Are the terraces of your hair where the dappled sunlight dances
We
In the fresh wind a door is opened
Countless hands that summon the green shades and us
The roads lie raw upon the soft earth's skin
In the spring-waters your arms gleam
And beneath our eyelashes, bathed in sunlight
Quietly the sea and fruits
Begin to ripen

(Memory and the Present, 1956)

On Place Names

Sing, O water mains
The waters flow through Ochanomizu (Water for the Shogun's Tea)
Collect in Kugenuma (Swan Marsh)
Descend into Ogikubo (Reed Hollow)
Glitter then in Oirase (Inner Rapids)

Sapporo
Valparaiso
Timbuktu
Keep growing like raindrops
In our ears
O spirits of all places
With strangely evocative names
Become a row of pillars in Time
And enclose me
Ah   Why should numbering all
The unseen lands
Fill a person thus
With clusters of music
As smoke gives form to the wind
Upon a blazing curtain
Names lend places an undulation
The names of places must be
Made of light
If you say "Venice" in a foreign tongue
You hear only dark waters whispering
Beneath lice-ridden beds
But ah, Venezia
If some auburn-haired girl far from her native place
Cries out   See
Light overflowing the Piazza's stones
Wind pregnant with doves
Ah
Look
The China Bridge of Seta
The China umbrellas and leather-soled sandals of old Edo
Tokyo
Always
Cloudy

(*The Poems of Makoto Ōoka*, 1968)

Chōfu V

To live in a town
Is to have some favorite place there.
Is to have some favorite person there.
If not, one shouldn't live there.

A child grows and grows
Yet the parent's unaware that he himself is growing older
One day he sees it in a flash and feels afraid
An alien encountered by the way, the Other that is oneself.

I've lost my way and drifted far
Yet have some favorite place there hid away.
Some favorite person hid away. Unacknowledged.
Thus, I am a paterfamilias.

But then one day, the nape of my son's neck as he silently reads
    the newspaper
Shows so delicate in the morning light
That I see and am struck with love.
Surprise akin to sorrow.
— Akkun! Will you too in time become "of draftable age"?

(*City of Water: Invisible Town*, 1981)

MASAMI HORIKAWA (1931–)

Fresh Pain-filled Days

Our sensibility is destined by the age.
When naked innocence is torn in two
From somewhere far beyond our arms' reach
Destiny assaults our core, imposing resolution.
But when we've drained ourselves, what will remain?

Terror and loving are one single thing
Who can face that day by day?
The spirit and a love affair are far apart
Within my sight the blue sky stretches on
The little pot set on the gas-range is wet and cool.

Lucky the one who can meet his real self
Even in the last moments
Shout. Be silent. Ghost, my ghost
When the sum of all you've done attacks
Will you bleed a bit, even you?

Drawing on all our strength to prop our egos up
Resisting our slow weakening
Deepening our sensibility as living creatures
Making up for the ever-bubbling cruelty and pity of things
Is all we can do.
But toward what sea are we heading?

The incision shines on the slippery slope of the word obscenity.
Shattering the time like glass with the ripened self
You chew through the ripened edge bit by bit.
When death and adventure are mixed and boiling over
The small stubborn balance of departure and return is stilled.

(Pacific Ocean, 1964)

KAZUKO SHIRAISHI (1931–)

Bird

Bye-bye blackbird
Hundreds of birds   thousands of birds   fly away
No, no   It's always one bird that flies away
From within me
Dangling my ugly innards
The bird
Each time I bear you within my body
My eyes are ruined   In blind darkness
I live in this world by smell
When I lose you   I see you for the first time
But then my life till now dies and
A new blind life begins to stir

Bye-bye blackbird   on the stage
He sings, completely turned into a bird
The audience becomes many tens of thousands of ears   pursuing
    this bird
The audience is then several millions of blind wings
The audience, unable to see
Flap their many wings and become bird-ghosts
Pursuing that single bird's voice there on the stage
They turn and turn among the auditorium's dim seats
But does anyone know   which is not a ghost
But a real bird?   Again
Bye-bye blackbird
What is it
That, in truth, flies away from here?
Even he who sings does not understand   All he does is
Sing his heart out, and feel what he feels
Now something flies away   That is sure
It may be his smoothest time

It may be his spirit's very tender tenderloin or
It may be a star's memory of a guilty sin or
It may be the fresh warm blood that pours from
The tulip-shaped brain of the child sitting right there in front

Bye-bye blackbird
I am a bird
Whether I try to deny myself
Or accept myself
This pointed beak that never stops pecking
These wings accustomed to flapping
So long as I cannot wrench them from myself
I am   today   a bird
I become a prayer   piercing the sky   several times a day
A bird thrust down from the sky and falling to earth
And I am the innards that support the bird that falls
They fell inside me   Gigantic birds
Small birds   from scrawny, difficult birds
To arrogant gentle birds
Some are but half alive, croaking
Daily I give these birds their bird-burials
On the other hand
Daily I warm the eggs of future birds
The more the eggs are those of monstrous birds that devour
      the future
The more I warm them with a desperate love
Bye-bye blackbird
I will let loose
The monstrous bird that devours me
Truly
I must let it loose until the blood gushes forth
While singing for it, with style
Bye-bye blackbird.

(*Tonight is Nasty*, 1965)

Penis (for Sumiko's birthday)

Maybe God is, though He seems not to be
And he is a humorist, thus
Resembling a certain type of human being

Recently
He came for a picnic
Passing over the horizon of my dream
Bringing with him a giant penis
Well
I did nothing special for Sumiko's birthday
How regrettable

I'd like at least to send along
The seed of the penis that God brought
To Sumiko's sweet distant little voice
There on the other end of the phone line
Forgive me, Sumiko
The penis grows bigger and bigger day by day
It's planted now right in the midst of the cosmos
Unmoving, like a broken-down bus
So
When you want to see some other man
Racing his car, hot woman by his side,
Along a highway with a gorgeous star-spangled night sky
Really
You must lean right out of that bus window
And take a good, good look
When the penis
Starts to move   and is there at the cosmos' edge
It's a splendid view   At such times
Sumiko
The loneliness of the starlit sky's radiance
The strange coldness of high noon
Goes to our guts
What's visible is seen, calm and clear
None can keep from going mad
A penis has no name, no individuality

And also, no date
So when, like a god-palanquin at a festival,
Someone goes bearing it by
In the midst of the uproar sometimes
One knows just where it is
In that confusion   at times
One hears a vastness of as-yet unknown violence and insults
From those seeds still not controlled by God

God, at any rate, is absent just now
Gone off somewhere, it seems,
Leaving only unpaid debts and a penis in his place

And now
A penis left behind, forgotten, by God
Comes walking toward us
Young, high-spirited
Filled with naive self-confidence
So that it resembles, in fact,
The shadow of a practiced smile

Penises grow without number
Without number they appear to walk toward us
But in fact it's a single one that comes walking on its own
Viewed from whatever horizon
It has, alike, no face, no words

That's the sort of thing, Sumiko
That I want to give you for your birthday
Covering your being with it so that
You cannot see yourself
At times you will become the very Will that is the penis
From endless wanderings
I'd hold you back with boundless love

(*Tonight is Nasty*, 1965)

TOSHIKAZU YASUMIZU (1931–)

The Bird – in four chapters

The bird saw a dream.
It saw a long long dream
That seemed endless.
It cannot fly away,
Trying to fly away
It flaps its wings and
Runs for its life
Yet always, always
It runs along the ground
Kicking up sand
Splashing into puddles
Running any which way
Yet always, always
It cannot leave the ground –
It saw a bitter, bitter dream.

★

Though asleep
Though asleep
The bird was in the sky.
Though awake
Though awake
The bird was in the sky.
Always
As always
Borne upon the wind
The bird was in the sky.
Far from land and water
Always
As always
It was flying.

★

Flying through
A cloudy sky
I can no longer see the distant lands
I thought I knew so well.
I can no longer see the log that floats downriver
The half that's dry
The half that's wet
Both halves
I can no longer see.
The hedges in a distant town.
A distant sky.
A distant heart.
In the end
No longer seeing these
I am flying
In a clouded mirror.

★

Of course
A bullet
May bring me down to earth.
Of course
Fatigue and the salt wind
May bring me down into the sea.
Of course
Habit and the season
May force me to return home.
But
Of course as well
I fly toward you.
Only that you are
Is certain
I simply fly toward you.

(*The Poems of Toshikazu Yasumizu*, 1958)

YASUO IRISAWA (1931–)

Untitled Song

When two lovers come together   meaning to die
    Jajanka   waiwai
The mountain breaks into a smile
Spews forth sulfurous smoke again
    Jajanka   waiwai

When the would-be suicides approach
Burnt Rock Mountain   where no birds sing
Weak sunlight   falls from the clouds
    Jajanka   waiwai
Falls from the clouds

When two lovers come together   meaning to die
The mountain breaks into a smile
    Jajanka   waiwai
Spews forth sulfurous smoke again

Burnt Rock Mountain   where no birds sing
    Jajanka   waiwai
When the would-be suicides approach it
Weak sunlight falls heavily on their spines
If you don't die together   the mountain will never forgive you
The mountain will never forgive you
    Jajanka   waiwai

Jajanka   jajanka
Jajanka   waiwai

(Happy or Unhappy, 1955)

Unidentified Flying Object

Even a tea-kettle
Just might fly through the sky.

A tea-kettle filled with water
Each night, softly stealing from the kitchen,
Over the town,
Over the fields, then over the next town
Tipping a little to one side,
Flying for all it's worth.

Below the Milky Way, below the lines of migrating geese,
Below the arcs of artificial satellites.
Gasping for breath, flying, flying
(Though of course it's not that fast)
In the end,
A lonely flower blooming singly in the desert
That white and favorite flower
It waters to the full and then comes home.

(*A Walk in Spring*, 1982)

Memories of Paradise

When the expedition arrived
Having crossed the long rise
Of flowering gorse
Our love was discovered
    in the late afternoon light
Then it was pinned down
In a specimen case
And – how to believe it?
Reported on at a learned conference

I was seventeen
And you –
With a ribbon in your hair, the color of the brandy
Glowing in my glass
    by the late afternoon light
Now (thirty years on) –
You were a girl of fourteen

(A Walk in Spring, 1982)

SHUNTARŌ TANIKAWA (1931–)

Sorrow

There where the sound of waves in that blue sky is heard
I seem to have lost
Something unspeakably precious

In the translucent station of the past
Standing before the lost-and-found
I became even more sorrowful

(*Two Billion Light Years of Loneliness*, 1952)

An Elaboration of the Way to My House

"Oh, a squirrel!" the girl screamed, dropping the fan she held in her hand.
>   —From "An Elaboration of the Way to My House"

The Marunouchi subway line is famous for running from
Ikebukuro in Toshima Ward to Ogikubo in Suginami Ward to
the southwest – a distance of no more than nine kilometers as
the bird flies – by an extremely circuitous route via Myōgadani,
Ochanomizu, Tokyo, Ginza, Yotsuya, and Shinjuku. My house is, I
regret to say, quite close to Minami Asagaya, the station just before
the end of the line at Ogikubo. When you come out of the station
at Minami Asagaya, you will unavoidably find yourself on a sidewalk
alongside the Ōme Road. If we assume that you start walking
east, you will find on the south side of the road the Suginami Post
Office and next to it the Suginami Police Station, and to the north
the Suginami Ward Office actually standing there; a little further on,
a shop selling sporting goods will, in this scenario, most likely catch
your attention. The correct thing is simply to turn right at that
corner, thus leaving the Ōme Road behind.

Going past the Suginami Waterworks Bureau without
making any turns worth mentioning, and descending a very slightly

inclined slope, you will find yourself directly facing the Asagaya Public Housing apartment complex. It's this route that makes that possible. Plus – though you may hardly credit it – the last several tens of meters will actually take you alongside a tennis court. Therefore, though you are to turn left as you face the apartment complex and then turn left again at the public telephone booth, the result is equivalent to going halfway around the tennis court. (You will, however, see to the right the Suginami Tax Office, after you have made the second turn to the left.)

The rest is very simple. Having turned at one of the small crossroads that you find in the area, you need not turn at the other one. You will probably encounter one or two commonplace tobacco shops, but there is no need whatsoever for you to lose your way in an area of this kind. There are no cliffs or man-made lakes or anything of the sort, so you can, as a matter of fact, ignore the possibility of danger. Having passed along the lane through the graveyard, you will at last see a vegetable seller's, which may serve as a landmark for you.

It goes without saying that next to the vegetable seller's is a liquor store, and next to it a sweets shop, then a dentist's, a paint shop, a bookshop, and a fruit seller's–thus forming a continuous area, a neighborhood-community. Crossing the Ōme Road to the north, you are in an area of ever-increasing building density that finally converges on the Asagaya National Railway Station. And, of course, from that station as well it is possible to reach my house after a short, leisurely walk.

(*Definitions*, 1975)

Mt. Yōkei

When I try to divide into lines words that keep on flowing like blood
    through my body
I can feel the words grow rigid
As if the words resented being touched by my mind

Opening the window, I can see the mountain I've been looking at for
    sixty years
The afternoon sun is falling on its ridgeline
As for the way to read its name
Whether I call it Takatsunagi-yama
Or Yōkei-zan
The mountain doesn't give a damn

But the words themselves seem ill at ease
That's because I know nothing about the mountain
Never been enveloped in mists there, never bitten by a snake
Always just gazing at it

I've never hated words but
Neither have I loved them
There are words that make me shudder with embarrassment
And words that, transparent, make me forget that they are words
And it can happen, too, that words carefully thought through
End in genocide

Our vanity powders over words
I want to see words' faces as they are
Their archaic smiles

(*An Innocent*, 1993)

HIROSHI IWATA (1932–)

A Hateful Song

Eight in the morning
Last night's dream
Slips through the door of the train
And sings this hateful song to us
"Drowsy? Drowsy, are you?
You want to sleep? Or not?"
Ah, hateful
Oh, hateful
We want to sleep but cannot
We cannot sleep but want to.
 Demanding daughter Bare barley
 Sly spirit and lessened love?
 Foursquare formality Ocean's urchins

Noon break
An old love
Dressed like a debt collector
Sings this hateful song to us
"Forgot? Forgot, have you?
Do you want to forget? Or not?"
Ah, hateful
Oh, hateful
We want to forget but cannot
We cannot forget but want to
 Demanding daughter Bare barley
 Sly spirit and lessened love
 Foursquare formality Ocean's urchins

Six in the evening
Tomorrow's wind
Extending a dark and gentle hand
Sings this hateful song to us
"Dreamed? Dreamed, did you?
Do you want to dream? Or not?"

Ah, hateful
Oh, hateful
We want to dream but cannot
We cannot dream but want to
    Demanding daughter   Bare barley
    Sly spirit and lessened love
    Foursquare formality   Ocean's urchins
    Ocean's urchins!

(A Hateful Song, 1959*)*

The Ordeal of the Animals

Deep in the blue sky
One brightly gleaming plane
A siren blares its stuttering sound
People hurry to kill the animals
Before the animals kill them
Mercifully and carefully

It was exactly eighteen years ago

The bear devours its snack and dies
Inside the snack nitric acid and strychnine
It eats its fill and dies

    Goodbye   dirty water and bundles of straw
    Eating   dependent   caged in
    That was my life

The lion dies at breakfast
In its morning meal nitric acid and strychnine
It eats its fill and dies

    Goodbye   dirty water and bundles of straw
    Eating   dependent   caged in
    That was my life

The elephant ate nothing
For thirty days   for forty days
Hungry, it dies

    Goodbye   dirty water and bundles of straw......

The tiger eats its evening meal and dies
In its evening meal too nitric acid and strychnine
It eats its fill and dies
    Goodbye   dirty water and......

The Indian python dies at the night-time meal
In its night-time meal nitric acid and strychnine
It eats its fill and dies
    Goodbye   dirty......

It was exactly eighteen years ago

Mercifully and carefully
Before the animals kill them
People hurry to kill the animals
A siren blares its stuttering sound
One brightly gleaming plane
Deep in the blue sky

(Intelligence War, 1962)

RYŌKO SHINDŌ (1932–)

The Plains

Past fields of sorghum   past pasturelands
Past fields of red poppies in glorious bloom
The grassy plains of summer
Spreading to the limits of the horizon
After the sun rose to its height
Its light, weakening through the afternoon
Dyed the whole sky and earth like blood, and melted into them
Then the moon spreads its radiance over the plains
For three whole days this scenery does not change
Each day   the sun rises from the horizon   the sun sets
Father   now
I go to meet you
Passing beyond the Great Wall
This wall that took two thousand years to build
I, who've lived but nine years
Now pass beyond it
The Great Wall's two thousand years
My nine years
Father's thirty-six years of life
Seem like illusions

The teacher with a stern look
Said "…so go home right away"
And the child in the next seat
Murmured
I'm glad it's not *my* father!
And then I burst out crying

Having seen so limitlessly wide a place
Having been covered by so huge an evening sun
Our   lives
Are smaller   than poppy seeds   I understand for the first time
This sky and earth swallowed up everything

I am not the only one who wept
The people of this land are weeping more!
Though our lives   are as evanescent
As a single tear   within eternity
On this beautiful globe people are drawn into wars
How futile!
Someday   these feelings
These plains   will be a bittersweet memory
Even after we have disappeared
Each day   the sun will rise   the sun will set
Father   I'll go on living!
Becoming a drop of blood I'll dye the earth
And flow into the sea
Till then I'll live   I'll live despite it all

Come   carry my blood
O train   O splendid Central Asian horse
To where my father is
Reduced to ashes

(*Stepping on Roses*, 1985)

SACHIKO YOSHIHARA (1932–2002)

Nonsense

The wind   is blowing
A tree   is standing
Ah   on such a night   it's standing – the tree

The wind   is blowing   a tree   is standing   there is a sound

Alone   in the bath   late at night
Soap bubbles   blown as from a crab   a bitter pleasure
A lukewarm bath

A slug   is creeping
Over the wet bathroom tiles
Ah   on such a night   it's creeping – the slug
I'll throw salt on you!
Then you'll be gone   yet still be there

Is it the being there
Or the not being there
That's terrifying?

Spring comes   again   the wind   is blowing   again
But I am a slug-in-salt   I've gone
I'm   nowhere

I must have been   buried in soap bubbles   and floated away

Ah   on such a night

(*Youth's Litany*, 1964)

TORIKO TAKARABE (1933–)

Field Notes at Bakoton, Kitsurin

During summer vacation in primary school days I traveled once
    with my father
So long ago, it now seems barely real
To a little village called Bakoton in the province of Kitsurin—
To the little village of "Bahutun"—
Father made my mother clip my girlish bangs
Until I emerged a lonely boy with nice short hair
And so
To this out-of-the-way place where bride-buying was still done
We went to study folkways
Two males together on a trip
Rowing a narrow boat with creaking oars
We crossed the Songhua River

It was a village of lovely willows
Made from the smells of water
Along the bank a crowd of villagers gazed at the foreign father and
    child
After many questions and answers
Father wrote in his field notes:
"Truly, this boat that looks so crudely made is a folkway unique to
the Manchurian people. It is made of elm, and takes two wood-
workers a full eight months to complete. Costing some two
hundred yen, each boat can be used for about four years, and a
boatman's daily earnings come to perhaps thirty yen per boat."

A child's small back, crouching on the riverbank to pass water
A village elder saw through my disguise and begged my father
To "sell this child as a bride for my son
Gold, silver, silks, a donkey—ask what you like"
"If the price is right, I might sell her"—Father replies with utter
    calm

Giving cigarettes to the villagers, he and the old man went down to
    the water's edge, sparkling in the sun
They began to bargain, counting out slim willow leaves as the
    custom was.
(In winter it would have been green beans instead. When talking
business, things that could not be divided were always used.)

With willow leaves clinging to his shoulders and back, Father
    returned alone
"The price offered was a thousand yen. Will you turn into a girl
    again, for that?
How about it?" he said, laughing.
Was this too, perhaps, a part of his folkways research?
So long ago, it now seems barely real
So I would not be abducted by the villagers
This thousand-yen girl
Father rushed me along—"We have to hurry"
On we walked, turning back to look at the white stucco corners of
    the village roofs

Around my father, the wet smell of blood
"You're a boy," he said to me
"Remember, you're a boy!"
I lit the cigarette he held between his lips
Near the riverbank waves rocked the boat
I jumped on board with a show of boyish liveliness
And as evening shadows crept along the river's edge
The waves slapped, mocking, at the shore

(*Slides from a Courtyard*, 1992)

TOSHIO NAKAE (1933–)

Night and Fish

The fish   at night
Feel as if they're floating out
Beyond the globe of earth
There is less water so
They swish their tails and fins
The night   is so quiet that
They worry about the sound of themselves splashing the water
Won't someone hear?
They peer into the night
And then they meet
A whirligig
That wandered off many years before
It's lost on its way back   and as if it had forgotten what to do
It's whirling round and round

(*Fish Time*, 1952)

Vocabulary Collection, Chapter 29

For Makoto Ōoka

a.

The dangling-on-a-scaffold scrotum

The old familiar scrotum
The none-too-bright scrotum
The stupid scrotum
The tried-its-luck scrotum

The blowing in the wind scrotum
The chilled by the snow scrotum
The burned by the sun scrotum
The faintly smiling scrotum

A young man's scrotum
A pus-exuding scrotum
A blood-dripping scrotum
A head-bowed scrotum

A nice fat scrotum
A highly talented scrotum
A retarded scrotum
A silent scrotum

An unfortunate scrotum
A still-living scrotum
A disgusted scrotum
An animal's scrotum

The ancestral scrotum
The paternal scrotum
The same old scrotum
The always-up-to-its-old-tricks scrotum

The dangling-on-a-scaffold scrotum

b.

The hard-working scrotum
The devoted scrotum
The busy-every-day scrotum
The contract-holding scrotum
The wiping its sweaty head and carrying to its girlfriend's
   storeroom a product quite different from what was ordered scrotum
The nonetheless totally sincere scrotum
The yet everywhere unloved scrotum
The sad, dusty, smelly scrotum
The working in total obscurity scrotum
The failed in business yet unhurriedly smiling scrotum
The calmly, coolly drunk scrotum   the screaming scrotum
The bold yet sensitive scrotum
The swinging as it wheedles scrotum
The strangler weeping and moaning at the cruelty of it all scrotum
The spirit and flesh scrotum
The illusion and reality scrotum
The two-faced and hence disliked scrotum
The shut out by its girlfriend scrotum

The never complaining about its work scrotum
The unconcerned about appearances scrotum
The apprentice boiler-stoker scrotum
The checking out the fire in its girlfriend's boiler scrotum
The caught between two thighs yet nonchalantly working scrotum
The serious scrotum   the joking scrotum
The utterly silly-looking scrotum
An old man's scrotum
An infant's scrotum   a just-born scrotum

(*Vocabulary Collection*, 1969)

MOTO'O ANDŌ (1934–)

A Difficult Walk

Remembering one leaf
Chasing after one leaf
And then   more deeply
Burrowing toward the muffled crying voice
Turning the rudder
Sliding over the incline
Cunningly imitating the growing tree
Longing for a more complex variation
Stacking cards, then breaking the deck
Crossing the river – a river
Without beginning or end it seems –
Still not forgetting the floating ice of ten years before
Until it melts
Warming it in the palm of the hand   smelling the fragrance
Fascinated by the young girls' ears
Spreading sand
Waiting for the birds to come and take it in their beaks
Waiting for evidence
Unable quite to accept the cold comfort
Letting the grass flow letting the voice flow
And then   once more
With head down crossing the river and coming back

(*Time in the Water,* 1978)

TAKU MIKI (1935–)

A Guest has Come

Today, a day when the world may be destroyed
In short   a commonplace afternoon
I see a little pillar of fire rising between my wife's thighs
At once she became a mother   and her husband became a father
No sirens sounded   the sky was not suddenly overcast
The mother only shed a few tears then slept
The father by her side ordered in "superior sushi" and drank a beer
At last she came   she came!
From amoeba through the stages of fish and fowl
Exhausting many storks on the way
Such a long long journey   You must be tired!
Welcome!
Kindly choosing   to come to a couple as poor as we
Thank you so much…
But the father, always prone to worry, is concerned
He can't help asking one after the other
—Hey, is your breathing okay?
—Your ears aren't blocked, are they?
If you've six fingers on each hand, you'll count by twelves
If four, by eights
My careless wife has doubtless
Made some blunder
Ah   but it's true   a human being
Just as all the books say   is born and gradually grows
Young girls and middle school students and grannies and cops
Snails and otters and "Blue General" snakes
Are no different from the elms in our back garden (it's really the
     landlord's, of course)
And I became a father too but
At the time   this newest-father-in-the-world
While imagining the weight of the giant milk-cans he'd soon be
     bringing in
In fact keeps his ears   pricked up

What he'd thought was the future suddenly splits apart
And beyond   an actual street appears
The cries that echoed across the dark sky
Before   from there
From now on are my throat's   are my new-born daughter's
For proof   just look at
The friendly glances thrown at this new father
By the people of the town
Those are   their frankincense and myrrh   so
By knowing what that means
I've now become a man who needs to speak of "hope"

(*Tokyo 3 a.m.*, 1966)

SHIRŌYASU SUZUKI (1935–)

Confessional-Fiction Virgin Kiki's Favorite Form of Play

From behind me at noon in the hateful mirror yellow Kiki
Comes
Then poetry becomes no good, a bore, a mess
If Kiki's appearance is my theme then there's nothing left to say
   (Note 1)
I'll have some fun with lively virgin Kiki!
Rolling the balls around, Kiki positions herself to enfold me
Kiki's body with its swelling expanse
Presses in on me
The old repeated sensation is mine alone
Existing as an individual I've nothing to fear
She's a virgin with parents so there's a point to our lewd acts
First I roll her skirt up
Fire in the forest, feel the excitement!
Women's toilet!
A virgin's crotch is a peaceful place and birds are playing there
From the smooth yellow cliff-face suddenly into the deep abyss
A pale love begins to bloom
I'll forget everything
I'll stop taking baths   (Note 2)
I'll stop working
Hunger makes one refrain from lying, they say
If I'm going to slack off it's got to be for Kiki
Going on a sentimental journey I take Kiki, now without her
   father, and sink her in lewdness
My penis breaks yellow Kiki's maidenhead and thrusts into the
   vermilion sanctuary
A trip with her swelling pudenda
After racing screams and laughter
It turns light and
Yellow Kiki, still in enfolding posture, grows more affectionate
Now her maidenhead's destiny has dawned – Felicitations!

Virgin Kiki gives my inner virgin's hair a good hard yank and kicks
    her aside
This is the reality of our idle peaceful journey
Virgin Kiki directly applies the much-talked-about Revolution
    as a dildo to my inner virgin
This is the reality of rolling the balls around
Night upon night of masturbation
This is our pointless poetry
Yesterday, a Sunday, Matsumoto came and talked of poetry   (Note 3)
He doesn't want to write poems anymore but
All the more seduced by poetry he only masturbates away
Such smugness
Will be the ruin of language, said I
So why don't I lend you virgin Kiki   (Note 4)
Anyway, that's the reality
There at the spot where she was taken away by Matsumoto, the cat
    is eating
As I wept, thinking of virgin Kiki's vermilion sanctuary
Somehow I wandered into the virgin forest of love   (Note 5)
Where have you gone, Kiki
I'm lonely, Kiki
I'm miserable, Kiki
It's too much, Kiki
Women are for lending, Kiki
Newly wed, Kiki
This is poetry, Kiki
Already despaired-of yellow Kiki
Oh, but
I ought never to have given Matsumoto Kiki
Uneasiness assailed me
Regret shook its head, cat-like
As it gobbled up my hairy heart   (Note 6)
Ah, then I saw yellow Kiki come back in front of the station
    (Note 7)
Ah, she's still a virgin
So at any rate for starters
I'll thrust my penis into the vermilion sanctuary, breaking
    yellow Kiki's enfolding maidenhead
Yet even so the finally restored maidenhead

The maidenhead that is Kiki begins to redden
With all-enfolding, rolling-the-balls-around joyful cries
I was raped from behind by the maidenhead
And unable to move
Ended up at noon as a peace-loving man in a men's toilet

Note 1   Kiki does not mean "crisis." She was often seen going to school in the usual way. She changed her clothes with the seasons in June and October. Her future is mapped out: there will be a wedding-ceremony, a family, sexual intercourse.

Note 2   When I was living in Misasa-machi in Hiroshima, I would go every night around 10:30 to the public bath. I would run or walk through the night streets together with my wife, washbowl in hand. On cold winter nights I wouldn't feel like going. If I'd say "I'm not in the mood," my wife would say "Well then, I'll go by myself." Being left behind would make me feel lonesome, so I would end by going along as well.

Note 3   I have no friend named Matsumoto.

Note 4   The idea of freely lending a woman intrigues me. But it seems as if something might get broken, so I just can't do it.

Note 5   The island of Miyajima, where Itsukushima Shrine is located, is covered in virgin forest.

Note 6   The word "heart" here means something like "nerve," as in "What a lot of nerve he's got!"

Note 7   The crowds of people that move about in front of train stations are, undeniably, crowds, and they give us an opportunity to realize concretely that human beings are animals.

(*Canned Life Together, Or, the Flight toward the Trap*, 1967)

The Name Sōta

And still the car with us in it
Followed the Susobana River
And climbed, making turn after dizzying turn
I worried that Sōta might spit up again
And he did
I felt Sōta's car-sickness in the pit of my stomach
At the tunnel exit
Vines hung down and glistened in the sun
We'd come into the mountains
There's lots of grass
With so much grass one's heart feels calm
That's why we'd called him "Sōta" [Many Grasses]
The grasses
Blown by the wind
Send their seeds aloft

(*The Family's Place in the Sun*, 1977)

TAEKO TOMIOKA (1935–)

Life Story

Papa and Mama
And the midwife
All the tipsters
Bet I'd be a boy and so
I made sure I'd break through the placenta
As a girl

Then
Since everybody was so disappointed
I turned into a boy
Then
Since everybody praised me
I turned into a girl
Then
Since everybody bullied me
I turned into a boy

I came of age and
My lover was a boy so
I had to turn into a girl
Then
Everybody except my lover
Said I'd turned into a girl so
For everyone except my lover
I turned into a boy
Feeling sorry for my lover too
I turned into a boy
But then he said he wouldn't sleep with me so
I turned into a girl

Meanwhile several centuries passed
Now
The poor broke out in bloody revolution
And were controlled by just a single piece of bread

So I turned into the medieval Church
Love, love, I said
And walked along the alleyways
Handing out old clothes and balls of rice

Meanwhile several centuries passed
Now
They said the Kingdom of God had come
And rich and poor were the greatest of friends
So
I showered calls to action
From my personal helicopter

Meanwhile several centuries passed
Now
The bloody revolutionary band
Were kneeling before a rusted cross
In the midst of disorder the flame of order could be seen
So
In some cellar bar
With Byron and Musset
And Villon and Baudelaire
And Hemingway and black-trousered girls
I played cards and drank
And argued earnestly
About Japan, that eastern land
And its own brand of libertine
We laughed at one another
About the simultaneity of love

Papa and Mama
And the midwife
All said I'd be a prodigy so
I was retarded
They said I was an idiot so
I became an intellectual and built a house out back
I had more physical strength than I could use
When I got famous
As the intellectual out back

I went out front and began to walk
The path was
Papa and Mama's path
The imp in me was at a loss
I swear on imp's honor I was anguished
So
I turned into a fine young girl
For my lover I turned into a boy
And permitted no complaints

(*Return Presents*, 1957)

Still Life

Your story's over
And by the way today
What kind of snack did you have?
Yesterday your mother said
I just want to die!
You took your mother's hand
Went outside together and took an aimless walk
You gazed at a river the color of sand
Gazed at a view with a river
Willows are called "trees of tears" in France, you know
The woman in the Bonnard painting said one time
Yesterday you said
When did you give birth to me, Mama?
Your mother said
I didn't give birth to anything alive

(*Women Friends*, 1964)

TAIJIRŌ AMAZAWA (1936–)

Morning River

Night turns many layered and collapses in the desert
Here and there enameled mourning banners snap in the wind
Nearby the river begins to shine with a faint blackness
Pregnant women emerge from the little shrine exposed to the wind
Their songs drift smoke-like through the air
They eat, scattering the cat's-eye morning like seeds
Yet when a line of brown-hued grass runs across the sky
The women at once cut off their own lips
And while cruelly trampling on the backs of men with their spiny
    ankles
Their whole bodies become earth-like hair and go in pursuit
Later the vomit of red grass blazes coldly
On the frozen walls leprous spots bloom
And the dregs of night brew dry whirlwinds
And amniotic fluid mixed with blood sometimes
Moistens a man's shabby little throat
In the sands of abandoned streets
Men's gray umbrellas will at last be lined up like a plague
On the sour afternoon pavements too
And on the river-bottom of collapsed trees eyes are thickly spread
And men once again dream of festivals
But the pregnant women will not return
The hazel-colored virgins more barren than a horse
Will do their best to keep far away from
The distant noontime waterway

(*Morning River*, 1961)

Counter-Western

Stride across the good-for-nothing river
The rays of sunlight shamelessly shine
Oh horizon of sneezes, snapping your fingers
We are a rank of fifteen thousand people

Lined up, mounted, on the riverbank
Hearing, enchanted, the bells' tolling
Between our thighs, meteorites
Little by little expand their shadows

Our half-transparent guns
Softly groaned, and we knew not what to do
The stars on the water's surface repelled us
With a dizzyingly dried-up malice
And what's more, the weak rays of sunlight, expanding and contracting
Drooled spittle on our cheeks
But we are a synonym for endurance
Those who could not be soothed melted their feet

Stride across the good-for-nothing river
The command raises its head from within ourselves
And links our insides with horsemeat
A tightened wire swells up at once
Our guns spew forth hot voices
The river that runs unsmiling past
The feet of this rank of people, fifteen thousand strong
Strikes our stomachs a dull blow

A hallucination of a slab of ice dyed in blood floating up
Our half-transparent flesh stagnating unevenly
One after the other explosions at every street corner
Make the birds' holes bloom
The rawness of the falling hillside roads, sliced off
A hot liquid pushes aside the river
And we, this single rank, fifteen thousand strong
Our bodies fused as one
Begin to walk, casting aside the tethered horses

We notice that it is a street of hot rain
Stride across the good-for-nothing river
We hear anew in the background the ranks of screams
The voices of our cruel children

(*Time Error*, 1966)

MUTSUO TAKAHASHI (1937–)

The Rose Tree

Oh my manly lover   you are a rose
A slightly pale rose   with the strong scent of sex
I   kneel before you
My trembling arms embrace you   your thighs are roses
Near my closed eyelids
There is a fragrant clump of grass
An infant rose filled with dew   sleeps the sleep of dawn
Above me, who clings to you   like some Greek supplicant,
With fingers dreamily extended   with jaw bent back
You   have become a sturdy rose tree
Its leaves are eating the sun

(*The Rose Tree, Imitation Lovers*, 1964)

Research on Weeds

"In the world of weeds
The struggle for existence is ever-present
There seem to be in particular some plants
That secrete a substance harmful to other plants"
As a middle-school student you stated this
In an essay printed on cheap mimeograph paper
Then you knew nothing about the spirits of plants
You didn't know about the spirit-substance
That the spirits of plants secrete from their spirit-bodies

    "It wasn't me
    It was my spirit that killed my younger brother
    So   I hope you'll punish not me but my spirit
    I'm guiltless"
    A criminal once appealed to the authorities
    If   the spirit of a person
    Is just a bit apart from the actual person
    Then the spirit of a tall goldenrod
    Is just a bit apart from the tall goldenrod itself
    The actions of the spirit of the tall goldenrod, however,
    Cannot but exert an influence
    On the tall goldenrod
    The actions of the spirit who killed the younger brother
    Sent the criminal himself to the gallows

Pushing through   the group of tall goldenrods
Swaying there just a bit apart from the spirit of the tall goldenrods
You went out into the world of men
There must have been a spirit swaying   just a bit apart from you
Was it you   or your spirit
Who wrote as follows in that same school-essay:
"This year there are far fewer spots
Full of tall goldenrods, compared to last
The substance that harms the other plants may, it seems,
Destroy the plant itself at that same time"

(The Rabbit Garden, 1987)

TETSUO SHIMIZU (1938–)

Charlie Brown

He moves back.
Chasing a center-fly
The boy Charlie Brown.
Just like the players in Casey Stengel's day.

This is a familiar sight.

She moves back.
Gazing at me in my suit,
The ninety-year-old lady Hatsukino Kame
Just as she did when she was seventy.

This too is a familiar sight.

With Snoopy along
There's no death for Charlie
With the molting chicken along
There's no death for the old lady
Since, like a piece of paper in a huge patch of sunlight
Her shadow has been melting in the grassroots all along.

Revisiting that hometown of mine
I touched my hands to the springtime waters after twenty years
Oh man in the waters! This too is an unfamiliar sight…
What have you been doing all alone, and where?
No matter how low you kneel there
Your living shadow is taller than the grass and so
Charlie will say
Hatsukino Kame will say
Would you get out of the way, please?
Having a creased bookmark
Inserted as we move back
Really bothers us.

(*Speech Balloons*, 1975)

RIE YOSHIYUKI (1939–2008)

The Blue Room

I am inside the blue room
What beats against the rain-doors is not the sound of rain
But the shrieks of an old madwoman
"Return my son   return my son"
They strike my walls and so
I shut the rain-doors tight and
I am inside the blue room

Will her son not come back?
I was not the woman   who hid him away
For only one can enter the blue room
It is endlessly blue
No coffin is here   no crematorium attendant to be seen

My son loved the color blue
He loved to gaze at the blue moon
At some point the blue moon and my son
Fell in love with one another
But on a night when his throat was parched beyond bearing
My son bit into the blue moon
That's why my son's blue moon no longer rises

They sent me word that
The dandelions had bloomed   and the wind...
So I opened the rain-doors   just a bit
The old madwoman was standing outside
She stood there   just to gaze at me

I am inside the blue room
That woman whose white fingers played the piano   long ago
Now pounds upon my rain-doors
"Return my son   return my son"

(*The Blue Room*, 1963)

YUKIO TSUJI (1939–2000)

Kameido

Nowhere to go
At the station
A notice says *poetry reading!*
So
What's so odd about
Me being beside Tenjin's holy pond
At a strange hour?
As I stand there silently the spirit of the place
(Wearing an old windbreaker and pushing a bicycle)
Sidles up to me and whispers:
At dawn, you know
Turtles and terrapins
Walk the streets near here
I've seen them myself
Three times

There've been a lot of changes in this town
That's given birth to a poet in the past but
No need to grieve
The alley that disappeared
Has only shifted to an inner place
With so many memories, so much loneliness
Hanging like wooden votive tablets
Softly clattering in the wind
Kameido Jūsangen Avenue
At the Suzuki ceramics shop the notice says *poetry reading!*
The open field of ragweed
Is the young Yasuyuki's, he who will become the poet Shirōyasu
In the shape of
A beggar chased away so that this rubble-strewn street may prosper
Or, of a forgotten wandering minstrel

(*Estuary Views*, 1993)

TAKAHIKO OKADA (1939–1997)

Borrowing the Name of Love Song

On a day when the rain pours down
Or, again, on a dried-up winter's day
I want you to say
"I've changed"
When I place my lips upon your pallid forehead
My lips turn blue
That such a thing as this is love
Even some wise sage
Would come and scold us
Let's at least rejoice that we were born in such an age as this
Won't you board the tram and go home, as always?
I'll wave my hand and look into your face, as always
Your brow shows sadness
My hair is too long
Sex is just not dirty enough so
I don't want to talk about it
The tale of you and me
Began with "I love you"
Our unclean natures fully on display but
It hasn't ended with "I hate you"
It's all a blur
I don't feel like going to the usual flower shop but
Let's just walk in silence to the station
Then I'll go off on a journey
Now too the flat sun will be covering that spot
In the dust-encrusted town
I'll develop resistance to gin and feelings
Become an ordinary company employee
Getting out of a standard-class train-car
In the Marunouchi business district, full of self-confidence
Because you will not love me anymore

(*Our Power 19*, 1963)

Endure the Splits and Wander On!

There is no need to hurry along the way.
Those who fear mistakes always perish.
The values that threaten your tomorrow are illusions.
If you freeze the wind into shadows
There is no need to hurry along the way
Shrinking back from vulgarity.
But you should deal vertically with reality.
Enduring the painful splits
Keep wandering over the non-existent wilderness.
Don't go for the easy way out, in your haste to look for roses.
Standing in the very presence of that which should be hidden
Enduring the split fork in the tree that's being pulled apart
That pain in your breast, which echoes without tears,
Let it deepen. Then
You will descend by yourself into the abyss of loneliness.
It is the river of death and so you can press on.
If, enduring, you've lost everything, say nothing.
Look at the birds that fly in a silence like the blue sky.
Be willingly deceived by a sought-for promise
There is no need to hurry along the way.

(My Eyes, 1972)

HIROSHI OSADA (1939–)

How to Eat Radish Wheels

With your own hands
You seize your day.
You seize a fresh day.
A day that's still new.
It should be a day like a good white radish
Lying with comfortable weight in the hand.

Then with a nice sharp knife
You slice the day cleanly into thick chunks.
You peel the day's skin right off
Plane off the corners, then
Into the unseen portions of the day
Make several deep cuts with the knife.

Then you toss it all into a deep pan.
You've spread dreams in the bottom,
You pour in just enough cold water to cover it and
Simmer slowly over a low flame.
Tenderly quietly you simmer your day
Until it's nice and hot.

Because it's a cold-hearted age, after all.
With your own hands, make of your day
A well-cooked radish
You need to eat it while it's hot and fragrant
From a heated bowl, with yuzu-miso sauce
Blowing on it as you eat.

(*Karmic Encounters Around the Table*, 1987)

AKIRA SHIMIZU (1940–)

Stranded Ship

Younger brother, lying asleep on your belly!
On your deep ocean
Does a stranded ship float
Like a song?
Against the backdrop of
My favorite, gentle poet
Coughing up blood
Flashed a voice-blow
Like a hatchet.
With what splendid terror did that dye the ocean?
Younger brother, lying asleep on your belly!
In the hometown that you hold tight
How many salty seamen's
Young oars
Are still thrashing the days' wind and rain?
What sort of girls are growing up
Drinking-in the tomato-colored twilight?
But I
Pray that you will not awake like me!
I
Think that to twist one's torso
And move straight ahead is the right posture but
Lately, somehow
My tongue flaps like a thin sheet of paper
At the slightest breeze
My head nods meaninglessly
Of course I no longer know my own age
And so sometimes
When I've drunk down the last of the sake
I'm overcome by intense thirst and
Alone on the stranded ship

Headed toward a dream unseen by anyone before
Like nothingness
Firmly
I settle in

(*Stranded Ship*, 1974)

GŌZŌ YOSHIMASU (1939–)

Burning

A golden sword looks directly at the sun
Ah
Pear blossoms that pass through the surface of a fixed star!

A wind blows
Through the Asian zone
The soul becomes a wheel, running upon the clouds

My will
Is to be blind
To become the sun and an apple
Not just to resemble
To become a breast, the sun, an apple, paper, pen, ink, dreams!
It needs to be a tremendous song
Tonight can you
Riding in a sports car
Crash straight into a meteor
And take its tattoo upon your face?
Can you?

(Golden Songs, 1970)

First Bath

Wet.
Wet. No one in this world has seen that. From the final sip of water to the first bath. From the first bath to the final sip of water. Mother! Forgetting that they are already so wet, when did you start to wet your eyelids? Tears spreading over your eyelids like signs of apparent death, Mother! Eyelashes! Rafts upon the shore!
Wet.
Alcoholic spirits, a forehead beaded with sweat, both are wet. The fabled continent that we've gotten used to calling the Black

Shore becomes visible to my eyes. It is not a rapidly flowing flood or deluge. Eyes that start to bud in some cracked riverbed are intimations. Mother! From the final sip of water to the first bath.

"A swimming corpse!" some yell, probably hungry ghosts from the village on the Other Shore.

Mother! They're very wet. The paper-windows, inner organs, insides of the head – all are so wet they're beyond help. Mother!

The universe is lightly bent, from somewhere comes the sound of water overflowing. Could it be the rainy season?

From the final sip of water to the first bath. From the first bath to the final sip of water.

What the hell's left for me to do?

A doctor applies his stethoscope to the body to determine if it's the rainy season or the dry.

Drip-drop. Drip-drop.

Drip-drop. Drip-drop.

The rivers and the lips are wet.

Is being a common laborer in a river-works project my occupation? I realize that I'm always left behind on a sandbar like the Milky Way, and the curtain of night goes down. Ah, Mother!

How I long for that familiar sea.

(*River, Written in Grass Script*, 1977)

MIKIRŌ SASAKI (1947–)

Rhododendron Hotel

The men are exploding dynamite all day in the mountains. It's to
build a road over the mountains. From time to time there is the
sound of explosions, and white smoke rises from the mountainside.
Shortly after, pieces of rubble fall into the river. The men
themselves are nowhere to be seen.

The women are gathered all day at the village pump doing
the laundry. They rub soap into the cloth on top of the rocks and
beat it. As they beat it, they mold the cloth like clay, turning it into
cubes. They press white foam from the cubes, and then rinse it away
in the water. They repeat this over and over.

The girls are lying side by side in the afternoon sunlight
on the large rock beside the hanging bridge. When they tire of
talking, they lie on top of one another. I couldn't hear their voices; I
saw from atop the cliff how each lay, covering another's body.

The boys are hiding among the rhododendron
bushes. Inhaling the smell of sulphur, they peer at the hot springs
pool on the river bank. From among the rocks puffs of red steam
come. There was once a giantess who tried to destroy this village;
she was killed by a monk who came from a lake to the south. The
giantess's heart was buried here, and even now pours forth blood. At
twilight a deer wandered into the water, dying the lower part of its
legs red.

A mound of stones in the center of the
village square. Mostly moss-covered. On the stones are carved
figures of deities riding the clouds. Looking closely, one sees
that these male and female deities are all embracing there upon
the clouds. The village sits beneath a giant crag. A crag that was
convulsed in ancient times. A gigantic stratum shook and emerged
above, distorted. Long ago the earth here moved like the clouds,
creating a heavenly pattern.

There's no one at the Rhododendron Hotel. The hotel is built on top of a cliff overlooking the village and is joined to the village by a hanging bridge that is tied to rhododendron bushes. In the hotel's garden, overgrown with grass, I washed my face and heated milk-soup. The villagers were watching me from the other bank. The shadows have no color. A wall of dung mixed with mud. From the window of the house surrounded by that wall, goats too were watching me.

The smell of a goat as it ambles along, its buttocks smeared with dung. The villagers make tea mixed with butter and salt in a wooden tube. The butter that sticks to their hands is rubbed on their faces. When night comes, all memories turn into smells and submerge. Together with the rain, wet by the rain, I opened my umbrella and crossed the hanging bridge that swayed in the wind. The camera's battery is weak. Sand mixes with my memories. I am forty-three. An age when no one looks at you anymore. The rhododendron flowers fell like mud.

(*The Honey Gatherer*, 1991)

YŌJI ARAKAWA (1949–)

The Greenery in Mitsuke

My gaze is green and low
Passing the greenery
On the way to Edo in Kaitai-chō

Mitsuke in the spring
O spots of green!
It's morning so
I will not pursue it deeply
Still
The grass is waving on high

My sister
Runs into the fresh green thicket
By the palace moat
Hiding her white thighs
The tremors of the wind at the leaf-tips' ends, and
The much lovelier sound
Of the endured slight spray
Strike for a time against the sounding undersides of the leaves

Having come running back
She cannot see me
It is somehow already
Dark and
The waves in the moat have ceased
The energy of my flesh as I move toward the woman
Has clearly made a path through the grass and
That alone is faintly visible

If we see dreams we can hide from one another again but, Sister!
Edo ended a while ago
And I since then
Have come a very very
Long way

Now I'm walking past the platinum gleam of the Saitama Bank, Shinjuku Branch. Noisy blasts of construction from buildings. Spray that quickly fades away. This colloquial age is cold. Seeking the warmth of the leaves' undersides, shall we set off once more, for Mitsuke?

(*Water Station*, 1975)

HIROMI ITŌ (1955–)

So as Not to Warp Them

I make little rice-flour dumplings and take them
To my man
I melt sugar and make the syrup
Place the boiled dumplings in it
And cool them
I seal them tightly in a bowl
And take them to him
The little dumplings stick to the bottom of the bowl
Their edges get torn
Their round
Shape gets warped
He scoops them up with a spoon
Oh
Watch out
Scoop them up
So they don't get warped
Dumplings, I love 'em!
My man raises them to his mouth
Mmm good! he shows by closing his eyes
I love 'em more than I do you
I watch him gulp the dumplings down
He slurps the watery syrup

I shake the bowl dry and wrap it in a cloth
And now we
Join our lips, tasting the liquid to the full
We slide our palms over each other's body
Giving shape to our love
But
You know
I don't want to be warped
I don't want to stay warped
That's what I feel, man, oh man of mine

I make them nice and round
Boil the dumplings, make the syrup, then cool
Sweet pain
I fill them with my yearnings
That thick syrup
Those smooth white dumplings
My man gulps them down
Thick as spittle
Smooth as buttocks
How do they taste?

I don't want to warp you
Sweetly pained, the man, too, felt
Done! My food, which I secrete
Into the man I love
Deep deep inside him

(*The Poetry of Hiromi Itō*, 1980)

LIST OF SOURCES

AMAZAWA, Taijirō. *Morning River* [Asa no kawa]. Tokyo: Kokubunsha, 1961.

_____. *Time Error* [Jikan sakugo]. Tokyo: Shichōsha, 1966.

ANDŌ, Moto'o. *Time in the Water* [Mizu no naka no saigetsu]. Tokyo: Shichōsha, 1978.

ANDŌ, Tsuguo. *CALENDRIER* [CALENDRIER]. Tokyo: Shichōsha, 1960.

ANZAI, Hitoshi. *A Handsome Man* [Binan]. Tokyo: Shōshinsha, 1958.

_____. *Cherry Tree in Leaf* [Ha no sakura]. Tokyo: Shōshinsha, 1961.

ARAKAWA, Yōji. *Water Station* [Mizu eki (Suieki)]. Tokyo: Shokishorin, 1975.

AYUKAWA, Nobuo. *The Poems of Nobuo Ayukawa, 1945–1955* [Ayukawa Nobuo shishū 1945–1955]. Tokyo: Arechi Shuppansha, 1955.

_____. *The Person on the Bridge* [Kyōjō no hito]. Tokyo: Shichōsha, 1963.

_____. *Shukurenkō* [Shukurenkō]. Tokyo: Shichōsha, 1978.

HASEGAWA, Ryūsei. *The Poetic Life* [Shiteki seikatsu]. Tokyo: Shichōsha, 1978.

HORIKAWA, Masami. *Pacific Ocean* [Taiheiyō]. Tokyo: Shichōsha, 1964.

IBARAGI, Noriko. *Invisible Deliveryman* [Mienai haitatsufu]. Tokyo: Iizuka Shoten, 1958.

_____. *It's Your Own Sensibility* [Jibun no kanjusei kurai]. Tokyo: Kashinsha, 1977.

IIJIMA, Kōichi. *Another's Sky* [Tanin no sora]. Tokyo: Yamanashi Shiruku Sentā Shuppanbu, 1971.

_____. *What Was Goya's First Name?* [Goya no fuasuto nēmu wa]. Tokyo: Seidosha, 1974.

_____. *Miyako* [Miyako]. Tokyo: Seidosha, 1979.

IRISAWA, Yasuo. *Happy or Unhappy* [Shiawase soretomo fushiawase]. Tokyo: Shoshi Yuriika, 1955.

_____. *A Walk in Spring* [Haru no sampo]. Tokyo: Seidosha, 1982.

ISHIGAKI, Rin. *Name-plates, Etc.* [Hyōsatsu nado]. Tokyo: Shichōsa, 1968.

ISHIHARA, Yoshirō. *Sancho Panza's Return* [Sancho pansa no kikyō].
Tokyo: Shichōsha, 1963.

_____. *Ashikaga* [Ashikaga]. Tokyo: Kashinsha, 1977.

ITŌ, Hiromi. *The Poetry of Hiromi Itō* [Itō Hiromi shishū]. Tokyo:
Shichōsha, 1980.

IWATA, Hiroshi. *A Hateful Song* [Iyana uta]. Tokyo: Shoshi Yuriika,
1959.

_____. *Intelligence War* [Zunō no sensō]. Tokyo: Shichōsha, 1962.

KAWASAKI, Hiroshi. *Swan* [Hakuchō]. Tokyo: Shoshi Yuriika, 1955.

_____. *How Trees Think* [Ki no kangaekata]. Tokyo: Kokubunsha,
1964.

_____. *Poems of Hiroshi Kawasaki* [Kawasaki Hiroshi shishū]. Tokyo:
Kokubunsha, 1968.

KISHIDA, Eriko. *Lion Stories* [Raion monogatari]. Tokyo: Shoshi
Yuriika, 1957.

_____. *Songs on a Bright Day* [Akarui hi no uta]. Tokyo: Seidosha,
1979.

KITAMURA, Tarō. *The Poems of Tarō Kitamura, 1947–1966.* [Kitamura
Tarō shishū, 1947–1966]. Tokyo: Shichōsha, 1966.

KIYO'OKA, Takayuki. *Frozen Flames* [Kōtta honoo]. Tokyo: Shoshi
Yuriika, 1959.

_____. *Sketches of the Four Seasons* [Shiki no suketchi]. Tokyo:
Shōbunsha, 1966.

_____. *Firm Buds* [Katai me]. Tokyo: Seidosha, 1975.

KURODA, Saburō. *To a Woman* [Hitori no onna ni]. Tokyo:
Shōshinsha, 1954.

_____. *With Little Yuri* [Chiisana Yuri to]. Tokyo: Shōshinsha, 1960.

_____. *Saburō Kuroda Poetry Anthology* [Teihon Kuroda Saburō
shishū]. Tokyo: Shōshinsha, 1970.

MIKI, Taku. *Tokyo 3 a.m.* [Tōkyō gozen sanji]. Tokyo: Shichōsha,
1966.

MIYOSHI, Toyoichirō. *Prisoner* [Shūjin]. Tokyo: Iwaya Shoten, 1949.

_____. *Poems of Toyoichirō Miyoshi* [Miyoshi Toyoichirō shishū].
Tokyo: Shichōsha, 1970.

NAKA, Tarō. *Music* [Ongaku]. Tokyo: Shichōsha, 1965.

NAKAE, Toshio. *Fish Time* [Sakana no naka no jikan]. Kyoto: Daiichi
Bungei Sha, 1952.

_____. *Vocabulary Collection* [Goishū]. Tokyo: Shichōsha, 1969.

NAKAGIRI, Masao. *Personnel Affairs* [Kaisha no jinji]. Tokyo: Shōbunsha, 1979.

NAKAMURA, Minoru. *Songs without Words* [Mugonka]. Tokyo: Shoshi Yuriika, 1950.

_____. *Trees* [Ki]. Tokyo: Shoshi Yuriika, 1954.

OIKAWA, Hitoshi. *The Rotgut Anthology* [Shōchū shishū]. Tokyo: Nihon Miraiha Hakkōjo, 1955.

OKADA, Takahiko. *Our Power 19* [Warera no chikara 19]. Tokyo: Shichōsha, 1963.

_____. *My Eyes* [Wagahitomi]. Tokyo: Shichōsha, 1972.

ŌOKA, Makoto. *Memory and the Present* [Kioku to genzai]. Tokyo: Shoshi Yuriika, 1956.

_____. *The Poems of Makoto Ōoka* [Ōoka Makoto shishū]. Tokyo: Shichōsha, 1968.

_____. *City of Water: Invisible Town* [Suifu: mienai machi]. Tokyo: Shichōsha, 1981.

OSADA, Hiroshi. *Karmic Encounters Around the Table* [Shokutaku ichigo ichie]. Tokyo: Shōbunsha, 1987.

SASAKI, Mikirō. *The Honey Gatherer* [Hachimitsutori]. Tokyo: Shoshi Yamada, 1991.

SEKINE, Hiroshi. *The One Who Promised* [Yakusoku shita hito]. Tokyo: Shichōsha, 1963.

_____. *A Single Strange Step* [Kitaina ippo]. Tokyo: Doyō Bijutsusha, 1989.

SHIBUSAWA, Takasuke. *Lacquer or Crystal Madness* [Urushi aruiwa suishō gurui]. Tokyo: Shichōsha, 1969.

_____. *Ode on Passing through Winter* [Ettōfu]. Tokyo: Shichōsha, 1977.

SHIMIZU, Akira. *Stranded Ship* [No no fune]. Tokyo: Kawade Shobō Shinsha, 1974.

SHIMIZU, Tetsuo. *Speech Balloons* [Supīchi barūn]. Tokyo: Shichōsha, 1975.

SHINDŌ, Ryōko. *Stepping on Roses* [Barafumi]. Tokyo: Shichōsha, 1985.

SHINKAWA, Kazue. *Not Metaphor* [Hiyu denaku]. Tokyo: Chikyū-sha, 1968.

_____. *13 Odes to the Earth* [Tsuchi e no ōdo 13]. Tokyo: San Rio Shuppan, 1974.

SHIRAISHI, Kazuko. *Tonight is Nasty* [Komban wa aramoyō]. Tokyo: Shichōsha, 1965.

SŌ, Sakon. *My Mother, Burning* [Moeru haha]. Tokyo: Yayoi Shobō, 1967.

SUZUKI, Shirōyasu. *Canned Life Together, Or, the Flight toward the Trap* [Kansei dōsei matawa kansei e no tōsō]. Tokyo: Kisetsusha, 1967.

_____. *The Family's Place in the Sun* [Kazoku no hidamari]. Tokyo: Shi no Sekaisha, 1977.

TADA, Chimako. *Festival Bonfire* [Hafuribi]. Tokyo: Ozawa Shoten, 1986.

TAKAHASHI, Mutsuo. *The Rose Tree, Imitation Lovers* [Bara no ki nise no koibitotachi]. Tokyo: Gendaishi Kōbō, 1964.

_____. *The Rabbit Garden* [Usagi no niwa]. Tokyo: Shoshi Yamada, 1987.

TAKARABE, Toriko. *Slides from a Courtyard* [Nakaniwa gentō hen]. Tokyo: Shichōsha, 1992.

TAMURA, Ryūichi. *Four Thousand Days and Nights* [Yonsen no hi to yoru]. Tokyo: Sōgensha, 1956.

_____. *A New Year's Letter* [Shinnen no tegami]. Tokyo: Seidosha, 1973.

TANIKAWA, Shuntarō. *Two Billion Light Years of Loneliness* [Nijūoku kōnen no kodoku]. Tokyo: Sōgensha, 1952.

_____. *Definitions* [Teigi]. Tokyo: Shichōsha, 1975.

_____. *An Innocent* [Seken shirazu]. Tokyo: Shichōsha, 1993.

TOMIOKA, Taeko. *Return Presents* [Henrei]. Tokyo: Private printing, 1957.

_____. *Women Friends* [Onna tomodachi]. Tokyo: Shichōsha, 1964.

TSUJI, Yukio. *Estuary Views* [Kakō chōbō]. Tokyo: Shoshi Yamada, 1993.

TSUJII, Takashi. *Poems of Takashi Tsujii* [Tsujii Takashi shishū]. Tokyo: Shichōsha, 1967.

YASUMIZU, Toshikazu. *The Poems of Toshikazu Yasumizu* [Yasumizu Toshikazu shishū]. Tokyo: Shichōsha, 1958.

YOSHIHARA, Sachiko. *Youth's Litany* [Yōnen rentō]. Tokyo: Rekiteisha, 1964.

YOSHIMASU, Gōzō. *Golden Songs* [Ōgon shihen]. Tokyo: Shichōsha, 1970.

_____. *River, Written in Grass Script* [Sōsho de kakareta kawa]. Tokyo: Shichōsha, 1977.

YOSHIMOTO, Taka'aki. *The Replica and the Mirror* [Mosha to kagami]. Tokyo: Shunjūsha, 1964.

_____. *The Complete Works of Taka'aki Yoshimoto, Vol. 1 Poetry* [Yoshimoto Taka'aki shishū]. Tokyo: Shichōsha, 1968.

YOSHINO, Hiroshi. *News* [Shōsoku]. Tokyo: Private printing, 1957.

_____. *Illusion, Method* [Maboroshi hōhō]. Tokyo: Iizuka Shoten, 1959.

_____. *When the Wind Blows* [Kaze ga fuku to]. Tokyo: Sanrio, 1977.

YOSHIOKA, Minoru. *Still-life* [Seibutsu]. Tokyo: Private printing, 1955.

_____. *Monks* [Sōryo]. Tokyo: Shoshi Yuriika, 1958.

_____. *Picking Saffron Flowers* [Safurantsumi]. Tokyo: Shichōsha, 1976.

YOSHIYUKI, Rie. *The Blue Room* [Aoi heya]. Tokyo: Bun'ensha, 1963.

INDEX OF POETS

Amazawa, Taijirō 116
Andō, Moto'o 106
Andō, Tsuguo 19
Anzai, Hitoshi 21
Arakawa, Yōji 132
Ayukawa, Nobuo 28

Hasegawa, Ryūsei 62
Horikawa, Masami 82

Ibaragi, Noriko 54
Iijima, Kōichi 72
Irisawa, Yasuo 89
Ishigaki, Rin 25
Ishihara, Yoshirō 3
Itō, Hiromi 134
Iwata, Hiroshi 95

Kawasaki, Hiroshi 68
Kishida, Eriko 64
Kitamura, Tarō 42
Kiyo'oka, Takayuki 39
Kuroda, Saburō 5

Miki, Taku 107
Miyoshi, Toyoichirō 33

Naka, Tarō 36
Nakae, Toshio 103
Nakagiri, Masao 20
Nakamura, Minoru 58

Oikawa, Hitoshi 1
Okada, Takahiko 123
Ōoka, Makoto 79
Osada, Hiroshi 125

Sasaki, Mikirō 130
Sekine, Hiroshi 23
Shibusawa, Takasuke 76
Shimizu, Akira 126
Shimizu, Tetsuo 120
Shindō, Ryōko 98
Shinkawa, Kazue 66
Shiraishi, Kazuko 83
Sō, Sakon 16
Suzuki, Shirōyasu 109

Tada, Chimako 75
Takahashi, Mutsuo 118
Takarabe, Toriko 101
Tamura, Ryūichi 45
Tanikawa, Shuntarō 92
Tomioka, Taeko 113
Tsuji, Yukio 122
Tsujii, Takashi 60

Yasumizu, Toshikazu 87
Yoshihara, Sachiko 100
Yoshimasu, Gōzō 128
Yoshimoto, Taka'aki 47
Yoshino, Hiroshi 50
Yoshioka, Minoru 9
Yoshiyuki, Rie 121

INDEX OF TITLES

A Crystal Madness 76
A Difficult Walk 106
A Guest has Come 107
A Hateful Song 95
A Morning Song at the Moored
    Boat Hotel 28
A Single Strange Step 24
A Tree's Fruit 57
Alabaster 39
An Ecstasy of Sloth 41
An Elaboration of the Way to My
    House 92
Ashikaga 4
At Tsukuda Ferry 48

Bird 83
Birthday 8
Borrowing the Name of Love Song
    123
Burning 128

Charlie Brown 120
Chōfu V 81
Confessional-Fiction Virgin Kiki's
    Favorite Form of Play 109
Counter-Western 116

Descent to a Singular World 47
Don't Bunch Me 66

Elevator Mornings 22
Endure the Splits and Wander On!
    124
Epithalamium 53
Etching 45
Evening Afterglow 51
Eyes Straight Ahead. Zigzagging. 1

Field Notes at Bakoton, Kitsurin 101
First Bath 128

First Dream of the New Year 75
For Spring 79
Fresh Pain-filled Days 82
Funeral Train 3

Heaven 30
How to Eat Radish Wheels 125

I Was Born 50
If Now You Suffer 32
In the Morning, the Phone Rings
    21
It's Your Own Sensibility 56

Kameido 122

Land / Houses 27
Leaving This Room 23
Life Story 113

Memories of Paradise 91
Monks 10
Morning Mirror 43
Morning River 116
Mother Tongue 73
Mt. Yōkei 94

Name-plates 26
Night 58
Night and Fish 103
Nonsense 100

Ode on Passing through Winter
    78
On Place Names 79
Our Song of a May Night 34

Penis (for Sumiko's birthday) 85
Personal History 16

Personnel Affairs 20
Picking Saffron Flowers 14
Prisoner 33

Rain 42
Research on Weeds 119
Rhododendron Hotel 130

Shijimi Clams 25
Sinking Temple 46
Sleet 19
So as Not to Warp Them 134
Song 67
Sorrow 92
Still Life 115
Stranded Ship 126
Swan 68

The Bet 5
The Bird – in four chapters 87
The Blue Room 121
The Gods of Poetry 46
The Greenery in Mitsuke 132
The Kite 59
The Laborer's Eyes 62

The Name Sōta 112
The Ordeal of the Animals 96
The Past 9
The Plains 98
The Roads of Miyakojima 74
The Rose Tree 118
The Sea of Sleep 37
The Soundless Girl 64
The White Horse 60
Three O'Clock on an Autumn
  Afternoon 7
Through the Ear 40
Tower 36

Understanding 72
Unidentified Flying Object 90
Untitled Song 89

Vocabulary Collection, Chapter
  29 104

Walls of Lead 71
Wedding March 69
When I Was at My Prettiest 54
Why Do Flowers Always 65